Praise for *Your Executive Coaching Solution*

"While targeting executives, Your Executive Coaching Solution *is a comprehensive and user-friendly road map for all members of the executive coaching partnership: executive, sponsoring organization, and coach. This substantive approach to executive coaching will raise the bar for what executives can and should expect. I highly recommend that executive-consumers, organizations, and coaches read and use this book so that all parties can reap the full benefits of executive coaching."*

—ROBERT G. GOODMAN, EDD, PRINCIPAL, RGOODMAN ASSOCIATES; FOUNDING BOARD MEMBER, THE EXECUTIVE COACHING FORUM; CLINICAL INSTRUCTOR, DEPARTMENT OF PSYCHIATRY, HARVARD MEDICAL SCHOOL

"Joan Kofodimos has created a sourcebook that is both a reflection on what constitutes coaching excellence and a road map to creating that excellence. I urge every coaching program to recommend this valuable new book to its students. Even better, I recommend that all coaches get a copy as a way of helping themselves maintain an overview of what really matters."

—DOROTHY E. SIMINOVITCH, PHD, MCC, CO-CHAIRPERSON AND DIRECTOR OF TRAINING, INTERNATIONAL GESTALT COACHING PROGRAM, GESTALT INSTITUTE OF CLEVELAND

YOUR EXECUTIVE COACHING SOLUTION

YOUR
EXECUTIVE
COACHING
SOLUTION

Getting Maximum Benefit from the Coaching Experience

JOAN KOFODIMOS

Davies-Black Publishing
Mountain View, California

Published by Davies-Black Publishing, a division of CPP, Inc., 1055 Joaquin Road, 2nd Floor, Mountain View, CA 94043; 800-624-1765.

Special discounts on bulk quantities of Davies-Black Publishing books are available to corporations, professional associations, and other organizations. For details, contact the Director of Marketing and Sales at Davies-Black Publishing: 650-691-9123; fax 650-623-9271.

Visit the Davies-Black Publishing Web site at www.daviesblack.com.

11 10 09 08 07 10 9 8 7 6 5 4 3 2 1

Printed in the United States of America

Library of Congress Cataloging-in-Publication Data
Kofodimos, Joan R.
    Your executive coaching solution : getting maximum benefit from the coaching experience / Joan Kofodimos.—1st ed.
        p. cm.
    Includes bibliographical references and index.
    ISBN 978-0-89106-221-9 (hard cover)
    1. Executive coaching. 2. Executives—Training of. 3. Leadership. 4. Executive ability.
        5. Interpersonal relations. I. Title.
    HD30.4.K64 2007
    658.4'07124—dc22
                                                                                    2007005233
FIRST EDITION
First printing 2007

To all the executives I've had the privilege to coach—you have been the catalysts for the development of many of the ideas and tools described in this book. I hope you all find your best, happiest, and most productive path.

Contents

Preface

I do executive coaching myself, and of course I'd love to promote it to people who read this book. But that's not my primary objective. The main reason I felt compelled to write this book is that, over the years, I have seen too many executives who received poor or no coaching, who missed opportunities to be more effective, and who struggled in their careers when something could have been done to help them. Consumers benefit more when they have a better understanding of what they're buying and how to use it. My purpose is to help people get the most from executive coaching, improve their performance, and enhance their career growth.

I'm in a unique position to produce the first comprehensive guide to executive coaching. Twenty-five years ago, before the term *executive coaching* even existed, I conducted pioneering research on executives at the Center for Creative Leadership® (CCL®), in Greensboro, North Carolina—learning about their character, their development needs, and the unique challenges they face. This research is cited as a key resource by the Executive Coaching Forum, a leading organization dedicated to providing knowledge about coaching, and is documented in several books and articles, which are referenced in the resources section at the end of the book. I was co-leader of the team that translated these insights into APEX, a coaching process for individual executive development, still used by CCL. I've presented this approach at several national conferences.

Since then, as a founding partner of Teleos Consulting, I have spent most of my career coaching executives and teaching human resources managers about coaching at companies such as Pfizer, General Electric, Merck, and Hewlett-Packard. I have also taught leadership and executive development at Duke University and the California School of Professional Psychology.

In addition, I am a recognized authority on the subject of work–life balance, which is often a key focus of executive coaching. I've published several books and articles on this topic, which are considered to be groundbreaking contributions. I've also been invited to speak at several national conferences and corporate meetings.

I have a specific viewpoint on the coaching process—as does every coach. However, while I will take different coaching styles and philosophies into account and sometimes use my own as an example, my job here is to describe a few universal principles necessary to ensure that coaching will help make executives more effective, and to minimize the potential risks to their success.

WHAT IS EXECUTIVE COACHING?

Broadly defined, executive coaching is a one-on-one consulting relationship dedicated to improving the leadership capability and performance of high-level managers. Increasingly recognized as a uniquely effective approach to development, it has become phenomenally popular in U.S. corporations. Surveys show that approximately 59 percent of corporations use coaches and that some ten thousand executive coaches are practicing in the United States today. Coaching has evolved from its primary use with "problem" executives into a status symbol for the enlightened or high-potential leader.

Coaching is popular for many reasons. It often helps executives change ingrained leadership behaviors, which few other development approaches can do. Moreover, senior executives value the privacy that a one-on-one development experience affords, and managers in increasingly lean organizations appreciate the opportunity to use expert help to develop their high-potential reports.

THE RISKS OF COACHING

Despite the explosion in interest, choosing and working with coaches can be a risky proposition. There are no generally accepted standards for membership in the coaching profession. A few organizations purport to screen and train potential coaches, but their authority is not widely accepted. Many individuals from related backgrounds have sought to enter the field; in addition to former human resources managers, management consultants, and therapists, there are coaches with backgrounds in sports, real estate, and even yoga. Of course, there are great coaches with unorthodox backgrounds, as well as ineffective coaches with the most sterling credentials. Unfortunately, there can be serious consequences from engaging an ineffective coach, ranging from wasting money and time to damaging careers.

The tension between executive coaching's immense popularity and its lack of clear standards has become a popular discussion topic, as evidenced by articles in the *New York Times, USA Today, Fast Company,* and *Fortune.* However, despite these concerns, a common discipline does exist and has been evolving for more than twenty-five years. The time is ripe to prepare executives to act as informed partners in the coaching process, rather than just as passive recipients.

AUDIENCE FOR THE BOOK

If you are an executive who is considering, or has initiated, a coaching process for yourself, you can use this book as a manual to guide you through the process. If you are a senior executive or human resources manager who is considering coaching for the managers in your organization, you can use it in making decisions about using coaching.

Your Executive Coaching Solution will help you

- Understand executive coaching, what it can accomplish, and what its limitations are

- Realize why specific strategies are necessary to overcome the special barriers to executives' development

- Decide whether coaching is likely to help you be more effective and successful

- Discover how to assess potential coaches and to choose the best coach for you

- Recognize the critical steps in a successful coaching process and learn how to manage those steps with your coach

- Learn not only how coaching can help you change your own behavior, but also how it can help you influence colleagues to see you the way you want to be seen

- Get the most from your coach, from the beginning to the end of the process

OVERVIEW OF THE CONTENTS

This book provides concrete information and specific action steps to help you get maximum benefit from your coaching experience, whether you are just considering coaching or are already working with a coach. It is divided into three parts. Part 1 will help you understand the potential value of coaching: how it works, what activities and outcomes are involved, and how coaching specifically addresses important hurdles in executives' development. Part 2 provides ideas and tools to help you decide whether you would benefit from coaching, and if so, how to choose the best coach for you. Part 3 focuses on the key steps in the coaching process, and the activities and results that should occur at each step.

Throughout the book, I provide examples from real executives, though their names and some specifics have been changed to protect their privacy. Each chapter includes supporting information, such as checklists, summary charts, and sample materials. Checklists will help you apply the principles to your situation. Summary charts will give you an easy way to remember the key points in each chapter. Sample materials will give you a concrete picture of various milestones in the coaching process. At the end of the book is a resources section with articles and books on specific topics and information about organizations working in this field, in case you want to investigate further.

Acknowledgments

Thanks to the colleagues who reviewed previous drafts and provided thoughtful comments, particularly Frank Kalgren, Len Rubin, and Ellen Wingard. Thanks to current and former Teleos staff who kept things going and allowed me to focus on this project: Lauren Gardinsky, Tracy Mallon, Sarah Howe Porco, Joy Shea, and Becky Stanco. Thanks to Connie Kallback and Laura Simonds at Davies-Black, who provided appreciation and guidance. Thanks to Bob Goodman for bringing the insights about adult development and perspective to our collaborations. Thanks to Kyle Dover for being an essential partner in the evolution of these methods. And thanks to Zoe Kofodimos for being so loving and so proud of her mom.

Part One

UNDERSTANDING
THE POTENTIAL VALUE
OF COACHING

1

The Meaning of Coaching

What It Involves and What It Accomplishes

The ultimate goal of executive coaching is to effect sustained change in an executive's behavior that improves performance. To achieve this goal, an executive coaching program must deliver on certain prerequisites, including providing insight into leadership behavior and style, clarifying purpose, improving relationships, broadening perspective, developing new leadership skills, enhancing ability to overcome barriers to change, and improving ability to learn. I'll describe each prerequisite here, along with the methods typically used to achieve it.

INSIGHT INTO YOUR LEADERSHIP BEHAVIOR AND STYLE

The first step in changing your behavior is to get a clear understanding of your current behavior and of how colleagues perceive you. Executives typically don't have an accurate picture of others' perceptions. As a result, executives often assume that their current approach is the right one and are blind to its downside. You are unlikely to change if you assume this, so it's important that you receive feedback about the effects of your style and actions.

Feedback highlights what you are currently doing and helps reveal who you are as a leader. Every leader has a basic style, which includes both inherent strengths and corresponding limitations. Style is important because it not only guides choices but also creates bias. For example, one executive we coached, Douglas Chen, was strong at establishing broad visions for the future. He saw this ability as the only important aspect of his leadership role because it was the one he preferred. He treated this focus as an organizational mandate, not realizing that his colleagues expected him to perform other critical roles such as translating his visions into concrete implications and ensuring their execution.

Furthermore, a person's natural style is unlikely to change, so any development effort must take it into account, building on strengths and compensating for limitations. Douglas Chen would always excel at visioning and struggle with implementation, but he could learn to value implementation and to rely on others to provide strength in that area.

How Can Coaching Help You Gain Insight?

The essential tool for increasing self-awareness is feedback, which can focus on a number of levels. First, it can describe concrete behavior and the impact of that behavior—intended or unintended—on others, as well as show you what you do that works well and what doesn't work so well. This kind of feedback usually comes from colleagues' reports about you. Second, feedback can reveal your underlying style, which includes fundamental attitudes, beliefs, patterns of behavior, thinking processes, preferences, wants and needs, and ways of learning. This kind of feedback usually comes from your results on psychological instruments or other tools geared toward assessing these dimensions of style.

CLARITY OF PURPOSE

Executives are often outer directed. In other words, their self-esteem is tied to satisfying others' expectations of them. If you are outer directed, you may lose touch with what you value and want for yourself. If you are required by someone else to enter into coaching, this can further drive you to try to satisfy a view of success that is not necessarily your own.

A basic premise of coaching is that how you lead is intimately connected to who you are as a person. To improve your leadership skills, you will need to strengthen your integrity in the true sense of the word: the connection between inner self and outer actions. To this end, the coaching process should help you clarify your true purpose, the value you wish to create in the world, and the principles you want to live by. This clarity can be a powerful tool to guide your daily decisions and actions.

In addition to lacking clarity of overall purpose, executives typically rush through their days not knowing what they want in every situation. Ed Romaine had this tendency. When faced with a problem to solve or a decision to make, he would ask others what they wanted, but he rarely stopped to consider or tell others what he wanted. As a result, he was well liked but not considered a strong leader, and he was frequently frustrated by the feeling that he wasn't meeting his own needs or achieving his goals.

The coaching process can help you clarify your purpose and identify your interests so that you can make decisions and choose actions that support them. It can also help you develop a powerful voice to advocate for your true interests. As a result, your leadership behavior becomes more intentional and you can decide how to act at every moment, rather than acting merely as a result of your history and programming.

How Can Coaching Help You Clarify Purpose?

The key tactic in identifying your purpose is to reflect on what drives your decisions and actions. This may sound simple, but executives rarely do it. True reflection requires you to take time and step away from the distractions that are probably continuous in your world. It also requires that you ask yourself (or that a coach ask you) what you are trying to create in your life and work, and why. You can find answers in a number of ways, such as through visioning, in which you place yourself in a future time and imagine what things you would like to be true of you and your world.

IMPROVED RELATIONSHIPS

Many executives are referred to coaching because of interpersonal behaviors that are believed to cause relationship problems. In fact, improving relationships is just as vital to the success of a coaching process as is improving performance. It's important to recognize that you are embedded in a web of relationships at work and that those relationships can either enhance or impede your effectiveness.

In addition to enhancing your effectiveness as a leader, improving your relationships will help modify others' perceptions of you. These perceptions are often biased by people's previous experiences with you, and others' preexisting judgments may be just as resistant to change as your own behavior. Involving colleagues in your development process can help melt those judgments and enable colleagues to see you differently. It also can prepare others to break out of their habitual ways of engaging with you, which in turn makes it easier for you to change your patterns of interaction with them.

Improved relationships can create stronger support for development. Typically, executives do not get valid feedback from their colleagues because these relationships are somewhat distant. If you engage key colleagues in your development process, you can counter this lack of feedback by sharing your insights and plans, discussing mutual expectations, and asking directly for support and continuing feedback. Involving colleagues in this way benefits them because it increases the chances that they will get the behavior they want from you, and it benefits you because it gives you the help and information you need to sustain your development.

Improved relationships help you accomplish your objectives because some of the behaviors that lead to improved relationships also enable you to influence others more effectively. Behaviors such as identifying and supporting your colleagues' interests could help build their commitment to joint projects.

How Can Coaching Help You Improve Relationships?

The main tactic for improving relationships is conducting planned conversations with colleagues. These conversations include both task-related interactions, where the coach can help you plan how you will behave in a way that is consistent with your desired principles, and developmental interactions, where you plan conversations with colleagues to discuss your development goals, ask for support and feedback, and establish agreements about how you will work together in the future.

BROADENED PERSPECTIVE

Some executives rise quite high in their organization due to their strong ability to conceptualize and think strategically, but they can become attached to the notion that their analyses and approaches are the best. George Watts was one such executive. He deprived others of any chance to develop or use their creativity, and he denigrated their contributions. He could not recognize that there are multiple correct answers in most situations, depending on one's goals and criteria. As a result, he lost influence and was stalled in his career.

Understanding this situation and others like it is a challenge of perspective. Executives' perspective—their ability to see and understand increasing complexity—can help explain both strengths and limitations. For example, one leader may use deep technical knowledge to develop brilliant ideas, but those ideas may not address needs that others perceive. To take the next developmental step, this leader must get past his internal definition of value to include the importance of others' wants and needs. Another leader may build great relationships with internal clients by meeting their needs, but may be reluctant to challenge those clients. Development for this leader involves going beyond the desire to please clients and instead learning how to influence them to achieve what would be most valuable to the entire organization. For each of these leaders, development requires a change of perspective.

How Can Coaching Help You Broaden Your Perspective?

The essential tool for helping broaden your perspective is the developmental coaching conversation. This conversation can diagnose your current perspective on a specific situation, and then use questions and observations to help you see different ways of looking at the situation. Repeated conversations can help you move from your current perspective (and its limits) to a broader perspective.

NEW LEADERSHIP SKILLS

Many people see acquiring new skills as the primary goal of leadership development. Skill building is critical, but it is difficult to build skills in a meaningful way without linking them to your unique purpose and style. As a result, skill building during a coaching process differs from traditional classroom-style training in two important ways.

First, learning skills is linked to role expectations. Many executives, especially if they are making the transition to a larger role, may not be clear about what is expected of them. What are the key activities they ought to address? Where should they focus their attention and energy? What is their purpose in relation to those above and below them in the organization? A skilled coach can help clarify roles, and as a result, critical skills become more apparent. For example, Suzanne Jacobs felt overwhelmed in her newly expanded role. She came to realize that she was involving herself too much in the content of her reports' work. Her coach helped her to identify key aspects of her role in relation to her reports such as establishing performance goals, managing performance in alignment with those goals, coaching them to develop their capabilities, helping them influence senior clients, and helping them resolve conflicts and roadblocks. These activities became the agenda for her skill development.

Second, in a personal coaching relationship, skill teaching can be tailored to particular styles and development goals. For example, Sid Galinsky was the leader of an information technology division in a utility company. He engaged a coaching firm to help his leadership team understand and implement his vision for how the division's focus had to shift in response to changes in the larger organization. Leadership team members participated in group training to learn skills for selling solutions to their clients, and the coaches helped them apply these skills in a way that fit their personal style. One member resisted Sid's expectation that he focus more energy on selling his ideas to clients because selling, to him, felt phony. The coach helped him develop a way to influence clients that felt natural and authentic.

How Can Coaching Help You Build Skills?

Sometimes an executive and coach will decide that the executive should attend a training program focused on relevant skills. Alternatively, the coach can teach skills individually to the executive or to an entire team. Either way, the critical part comes afterward, when the skills are applied to real-life situations and challenges through coaching conversations. Your coach will work with you to plan how to approach the situation and apply your skills and then will debrief your actions after you have carried out the plan.

ABILITY TO IDENTIFY AND OVERCOME BARRIERS TO CHANGE

Ultimately, you must incorporate the desired changes into your repertoire in a way that lasts. Such change should occur over time, as the coach assists with implementation. The coach will help you practice new behaviors in a structured way and build skills gradually. You and your coach will have to deal with the inevitable resistance that occurs as you try to unlearn deeply rooted habits and learn new ones.

When you try new behaviors, they will sometimes feel difficult or uncomfortable, and you may feel you do not perform them skillfully. In addition, under stress, you may revert to old behaviors. When these things happen, it is important to identify the roadblocks that arise from your personality: the patterns of belief, emotion, and attitude that can block desired behaviors and trap you in old patterns. The roadblocks may never totally disappear, but over time you can learn to anticipate them and make different choices aligned with your interests. For example, Allen Goldstein was working on listening to others' perspectives and accepting that he didn't always have the right answer. Although he was improving, Allen realized that when he believed others were challenging him, he slipped back into an old defensive and self-righteous mode. He learned to recognize that feeling and use it as a red flag; whenever he experienced that feeling, he would begin observing himself and focusing on asking questions rather than defending himself.

How Can Coaching Help You Identify and Overcome Barriers to Change?

It is important to discuss roadblocks and backsliding with your coach when you discover them. The coach will work with you to understand these issues and to develop strategies for avoiding them in the future, by creating specific plans and scripts to replace the habitual ones.

IMPROVED ABILITY TO LEARN

If you remain dependent on your coach to get you feedback and help you learn, then your coach has done you a disservice. An important goal of the coaching process is to help you internalize the ability to learn and grow continuously. To sustain improvements in behavior and results, you must be able to modify your style and behavior in response to changing situations and demands. The ability to learn involves being able to step back at any moment, identify your own and others' interests, and choose actions that will satisfy all those interests. It also involves reflecting on your actions and their effects, seeking feedback from others about your impact, and modifying subsequent actions on the basis of this information.

How Can Coaching Help You Learn?

The coach uses a cyclical process that includes identifying your interests, understanding your current style and desired behaviors, planning interactions, carrying them out, debriefing the results, and identifying implications for future actions. If the coach makes this process explicit over the course of the coaching engagement, you can become more skilled at moving through the entire cycle on your own.

You may be wondering why you have to accomplish all these prerequisites to perform better as a leader, and why you would choose to engage in an intensive—and expensive—process like coaching in order to accomplish them. Can't you just go to a training program or ask for feedback on a paper-and-pencil leadership survey? In the next chapter I'll explain why not.

SUMMARY

How Coaching Activities Lead to Outcomes That Support Improved Performance

COACHING ACTIVITIES	INTENDED OUTCOMES FOR EXECUTIVE
Procuring and providing others' feedback on: • Executive's behavior and impact • Executive's style	**Increased insight on:** • Behavior and impact • Strengths and limitations • Style: patterns and preferences
Facilitating structured reflection to clarify: • Executive's purpose, vision • Executive's interests in any situation	**Clearer purpose, which enables:** • Integrity between values and behavior • Ability to choose actions aligned with intentions
Facilitating interactions with stakeholders on: • Mutual tasks • Executive's development	**Improved relationships, which result in:** • Revised perceptions of executive by key stakeholders • Support for executive's development • Stronger ability to influence others
Conducting developmental conversations to surface: • Executive's current perspective • Potential alternative perspectives	**Broader perspective:** • Ability to take multiple perspectives • Ability to create broader value
Teaching skills that are: • Relevant to executive's role • Tailored to executive's style	**Acquisition of skills and knowledge:** • Understanding of leadership role • Ability to carry out key leadership tasks
Structuring implementation through: • Planned interactions • Debriefed interactions	**Self-directed development** • Ability to get feedback • Ability to assess progress • Ability to reflect on interactions

2

The Value
of Coaching

Why It Works When Other Development Efforts May Not

This chapter explains why intensive methods such as coaching are necessary, and why simply attending a training program or getting feedback from a survey won't create real and sustainable improvement in your leadership effectiveness. The chapter addresses the special challenges to executives' development and what a development process must include to have a meaningful impact.

WHAT MAKES EXECUTIVE DEVELOPMENT CHALLENGING?

Challenges in executive development come from both the job itself and the person. Job challenges concern the power and pressures of the executive position. Personal challenges concern the type of person who tends to seek and achieve a high-level position. There are five key challenges: lack of authentic feedback, lack of time for and value placed on reflection, reluctance to reveal weaknesses to others, reluctance to acknowledge weaknesses to oneself, and fear of letting go of a (previously) successful style.

Lack of Authentic Feedback

The more authority you have, the less likely you are to get authentic feedback. Others will be reluctant to give you feedback they perceive to be critical of your style or behavior. This reluctance exists for several reasons. First, you may present an air of authority and dominance that discourages any kind of interaction that could be construed as a challenge. You may not even realize that you have this effect on others. You may have an abrasive style that makes others fear retribution if they challenge you, or you may convey an attitude of superiority that they find intimidating.

Second, you may feel—as many executives do—that others are scrutinizing your every action or comment. If so, you may become very cautious about what you say or do. This can further increase the distance in relationships with those around you and minimize any chance of casual interchange.

Third, you may have become isolated from all but a small "brain trust." The members of this brain trust can compound your isolation by trying to protect you from distractions and annoyances.

Fourth, you may have surrounded yourself with people who are just like you and thus are blind to your limitations. Or finally, you may have the power to ignore any mandates to solicit performance evaluations from your colleagues.

The consequence is that you may have a narrow or distorted view of how you are perceived and how your behavior affects others. Research has shown, though, that executives whose self-perception is very different from others' perceptions of them are less effective than those whose self-perception matches others' perceptions. Without an accurate picture, you may assume that there are no negative consequences of your behavior, or you may focus your development on the wrong things.

Lack of Time for and Value Placed on Reflection

In addition to receiving feedback from others, you could understand yourself better by reflecting on how you've acted in various situations and how others have reacted. But the nature of your work makes this difficult to accomplish. If you are like most executives, you face enormous, continuous, and widely varying demands on your time—demands that appear suddenly and require immediate action. In addition, you may not value reflection if you don't see its relevance to your work performance. You may feel that you need to be focused on action, on tangible results, and the link between your behavior and results may not be immediately evident. As a consequence, you may not recognize when your behavior may hinder results or conflict with your values. For example, George Watts was referred to coaching because of his autocratic and abrasive style, which he felt was necessary to drive his staff to the brilliant analyses for which his boss amply rewarded him. However, he didn't realize that the pressure he put on others to do things his way was counterproductive—that it caused others to feel coerced, so they found ways to sabotage his mandates. Furthermore, George sometimes found himself suppressing the bothersome feeling that his autocratic style was at odds with his strong religious values.

Reluctance to Reveal Weaknesses to Others

Despite the barriers, executives do get authentic feedback now and then. However, for this feedback to be useful, they must be willing to consider its validity and also acknowledge the need for change. If you're like many executives, you may be reluctant to express a need for personal improvement. Part of this reluctance is due to the pressures of your environment. Other organization members may expect you to be invulnerable, like a parent they can rely on to always do the right thing and protect them from harm. As well, demonstrating your weaknesses to outsiders may have a material effect on investors' and analysts' confidence in the organization. The perks and treatment you receive can reinforce these pressures by sending a message that you'd better live up to others' high expectations.

The reluctance to acknowledge weaknesses or vulnerability is also related to the typical "mastery-oriented" executive personality. If you're mastery oriented, you seek to project a strong and competent image, and you're concerned about being seen as wrong or imperfect. You don't want to be seen as needing development help because this may bring disapproval from others or may make you appear weak or vulnerable. This concern is one reason senior executives tend to avoid public training programs, unless they are focused on safer intellectual topics, such as the programs at Aspen Institute or Harvard Business School.

Reluctance to Acknowledge Weaknesses to Oneself

Not only might you avoid letting others see your vulnerability, but you might also avoid acknowledging it to yourself, including the possibility that you need development help. You may hold a strong conviction that your perspectives and approaches are fine and may find it scary to consider the idea that you are not always right. Also, depending on where you focus your attention, you may not see a need for change. If what you care about is satisfying your bosses, and they are happy with your behavior and performance, then you may not be concerned about the fact that your direct reports aren't as happy. Similarly, if you believe your behavior is leading to positive business results, you may not care so much if there are concerns about your interpersonal style. You may see these concerns as an acceptable cost for achieving results that are more valued by others.

Fear of Letting Go of a (Previously) Successful Style

You may fear that, if you modify your style, you risk losing your effectiveness. After all, your current style has worked quite well for you! Tom Alessandro had received feedback that he was overly involved in detail and needed to step back and lead at a broader level. At one point, he telephoned his coach in great frustration, saying, "I used to be so certain of what I had to do in any given situation. Now

I'm second-guessing myself so much, I don't know how to act half the time!" In other words, letting go of your tried-and-true strategies and trying something different can make you feel vulnerable and out of control—a feeling you aren't likely to enjoy. Sometimes the reluctance to change is reflected in a kind of self-sealing logic in which you decide that the capabilities you need to develop are those at which you are already strong, thus devaluing those in which you have limitations.

COACHING STRATEGIES FOR SUCCESSFUL DEVELOPMENT

These challenges to development suggest certain strategies for increasing the likelihood of success of development efforts. These strategies include procuring and providing authentic feedback, making the benefits of behavior change compelling, designing a path to behavior change, ensuring privacy, involving others, and linking training to real-life challenges—all of which are essential elements of executive coaching.

Procuring and Providing Authentic Feedback

It's necessary for you to receive accurate, concrete information about your actual behavior and its consequences—consequences to which you are likely to have been blind. It's also necessary to provide safety for those who are giving you feedback, to overcome the self-censorship caused by fear. Confidential interviews or pencil-and-paper instruments can help create a feeling of safety, but be aware that not all feedback is created equal. Pencil-and-paper feedback instruments have grown popular, and many organizations are using them wholesale on their entire executive population. There is a place for these instruments, but a number on a scale by itself is unlikely to give you a clear picture of your behavior and its impact. What's most useful is concrete information about what you have done in specific situations and what effect you caused. This type of information—both candid and in context—can usually be obtained only by an external third party who is not involved with performance or appraisal processes.

Making the Benefits of Behavior Change Compelling

You will overcome the barriers to development only if you see benefits from it. Your internal defenses will find many creative ways to convince you that you need not, or should not, change. The best chance of helping you see the benefits of change is in a one-on-one relationship, where the coach can help you see how your behavior may be violating your own values or blocking the path to the outcomes you most care about.

Designing a Path to Behavior Change

Even if you accept the issues raised by feedback as valid and acknowledge that you could be doing some things differently, you are unlikely to find a path to changing your behavior on your own. In a choice between the familiar (even if dysfunctional) and the unfamiliar, most executives return to the familiar. In addition, you may not know which new behaviors will lead to achieving your goals. Coaching can help you identify actual work situations and relationships where you can focus your development efforts, think of concrete ways to change your behavior that support your development goals, and supply you with concrete scripts and tactics for the new behaviors you wish to implement.

Ensuring Your Privacy

Ultimately, to continue growing and changing, you will need to risk being publicly vulnerable. However, especially in the beginning, you may feel that your development efforts should be kept private. The coaching relationship provides you with a confidential setting for discussing weaknesses and trying new behaviors. From that starting point, you can gradually choose riskier situations and relationships for applying the new behaviors.

Helping You Involve Others

You can't do your job in isolation, and you can't develop in isolation either. The relationship with your coach is just one of the relationships that can help you. You also need to involve your colleagues, by getting their feedback, talking with them about your development and their expectations of you, and enlisting their support. Involving colleagues can help you see that they too struggle with development issues, and you are likely to feel less alone as a result. This step not only helps you change but also helps others alter their judgments about your leadership.

Linking Your Development to Real-Life Challenges

Training programs can help you learn new theories or skills. Unfortunately, you are unlikely to incorporate these new skills or models into your on-the-job behavior unless two conditions are met. First, you must get some idea of how your style intersects with the skills or models being taught and how the skills can address real issues in your performance. Second, training must be supported with hands-on coaching that helps you translate new skills into your day-to-day actions and helps you overcome the barriers to change.

OK, so now you understand the rationale for coaching. How do you make a decision about whether to embark on a coaching project yourself, and if you decide to do so, how do you choose a coach? Part 2 will help you get started on the decision-making path.

SUMMARY

How Coaching Addresses the Challenges to the Executive's Development

CHALLENGES TO EXECUTIVE'S DEVELOPMENT	WHAT COACHES DO TO HELP OVERCOME THE CHALLENGES
Lack of authentic feedback, due to: • Intimidating demeanor • Distance in relationships • Isolation	**Procure and provide authentic feedback by:** • Ensuring a confidential setting • Using specific descriptions of behavior
Lack of time for and value placed on reflection, due to: • Intense job demands • Focus on results	**Make the benefits of change compelling by:** • Revealing how behavior conflicts with values • Revealing how behavior impedes desired outcomes
Reluctance to reveal weaknesses to others, due to: • External pressure to appear strong • Internal desire to appear strong	**Design a path to behavior change by:** • Suggesting behaviors that will support desired outcomes • Creating scripts that put new behaviors into practice
Reluctance to acknowledge weaknesses to oneself, due to: • Need to feel right • Focus on outcomes rewarded by others	**Ensure executive's privacy by:** • Creating confidential space to discuss weaknesses and practice skills • Expanding efforts gradually to riskier areas and relationships
Fear of letting go of a successful style, due to: • Risk of losing effectiveness • Discomfort of uncertainty	**Teach executive to involve colleagues by:** • Sharing information about executive's development efforts • Enlisting colleagues' feedback and support
	Link development to real-life challenges by: • Tailoring skills to executive's individual style • Getting executive to apply skills to daily work

Part Two

MAKING THE DECISION
ABOUT COACHING

3

When to Use Coaching

Situations in Which Coaching May—or May Not—Improve Effectiveness

One of the first things you will have to do is decide whether executive coaching can help you address your specific challenges. Over the years, I've seen executives look to coaching to address all kinds of situations. The success or failure of a coaching effort depends on three major variables: the nature of your development needs, your readiness as a client, and the willingness of key colleagues to engage in the process. As you begin reading, you may want to reflect on these variables in your particular situation to decide whether coaching can help you reach your goals.

THE NATURE OF YOUR DEVELOPMENT NEEDS

The specific nature of your development needs is probably the first aspect to consider when deciding whether coaching will have an impact. It is important to know what your specific development needs are, as they will shape the coaching approach. Typically, people approach coaches to address performance issues, support their transition needs, or enhance their strategic effectiveness.

Addressing Your Performance Issues

Sponsors (usually bosses or human resources managers) traditionally seek coaching when they are faced with an executive whose behavior is troubling in some way, but who also contributes significant value to the organization. Often, behaviors that are seen as troubling in the current role are the same ones that were rewarded at lower organization levels or in past cultures that have fallen out of favor. In such situations, sponsors usually believe that the executive is unaware of the negative consequences of the behavior.

Sponsors have turned to coaching to help executives reduce interpersonal abrasiveness, stop micromanaging, address customer dissatisfaction, manage change more effectively, and improve poor execution—all in an attempt to preserve the organization's investment in the executive.

Interpersonal abrasiveness. George Watts had moved far in management at a relatively young age. Although his bosses admired his strategic judgment and problem-solving ability, his style of working with others was sometimes a problem. He was highly directive and, convinced that he was always right, often discounted others' contributions. Peers saw his behavior as abrasive and demeaning. As a result, he had difficulty working with other powerful people or building support for his ideas.

Micromanagement. Tom Alessandro, a senior executive in charge of a billion-dollar business, had an extremely hands-on style. He was reluctant to let go of even the most minor decisions. As a result, co-workers were stalled while waiting for him to get to their issues, and he was working twenty-hour days. He wanted to create a more empowering culture and to stop being the bottleneck for decisions, but he didn't know how.

Customer dissatisfaction. Kay Bradford was the head of a contract manufacturing group whose client ran a retail business. Her boss initiated coaching because this client complained that Kay was not addressing his needs. He saw her as passive and tactically focused and wanted her to be more proactive and develop strategies that would help him achieve his sales and profit goals.

Managing change more effectively. Allen Goldstein was brought into a large manufacturing company to lead a technological change in support of the company's strategic initiatives. He did this so aggressively, and with such little regard for others' input, that his efforts generated considerable backlash and tension. Without the support and commitment of organization members, the success of his effort was endangered.

Improving poor execution. Douglas Chen was a brilliant and creative marketing executive. However, his performance was criticized by his management, who claimed that he was unable to turn his visions into reality and that he provided broad plans when details and figures were expected.

In each of these situations, regardless of the executive's particular combination of strengths and limitations, coaching was able to help him or her understand what was blocking effectiveness and then address the issues. However, certain challenges can arise when executives perceived as having performance problems are asked to participate in coaching. Ironically, this traditional rationale for coaching also carries the greatest risks. These risks come from both the executives' reluctance to engage and other colleagues' unwillingness to support the process.

Sometimes—but by no means always—executives who have been labeled as having performance problems will be highly resistant to change. Often, such people are referred to coaches only when internal feedback and development efforts have not produced the desired effect. Some resistance can be a normal reaction to the pressure of external forces. In the extreme case, it can be a sign of psychological issues that are beyond the scope of coaching.

Another equally important challenge has to do with the ingrained perceptions and expectations of stakeholders. Often, by the time an executive with performance problems is referred to a coach, the sponsor has become frustrated and is close to concluding that the executive can't improve. Only dramatic and quick changes will satisfy the sponsor, and under the circumstances this degree of change is unlikely. Any evidence of the old behaviors simply confirms the sponsor's suspicion that the executive really can't change, often despite clear evidence of new behavior. In a sense, hiring coaches serves as due diligence to justify terminating executives, although few sponsors ever acknowledge this.

Even when executives and others want change to happen and are willing to try, sometimes the gap between the demands of a particular role and an executive's natural style is just too large. Sponsors may seek coaching as a last-ditch effort, but unfortunately coaching cannot completely transform a deep-rooted character.

This is not to say that those dealing with performance issues should not engage in coaching. But if the choice is made to engage, in the initial contracting phase there should be an explicit test of each party's willingness to change, detailed expectations of everyone's participation, and a shared understanding of both desired and likely outcomes. (See Chapter 5 for more information on contracting.)

The risks of coaching in a situation where stakeholders perceive that executives have performance problems include the following:

- Colleagues' perceptions may be permanently set.

- Simply initiating a coaching process can heighten expectations of change beyond what's possible.

- An executive who needs to be "fixed" is likely to have heightened defensiveness and to resist change.

- An executive who is perceived as needing "fixing" may fundamentally lack fit in his or her role.

- Once a problem has been labeled as residing in the executive, others may be unwilling to consider that there may be other contributions to the problem, including their own.

Increasingly, management is seeking coaching for situations other than those involving performance problems. Organization members tend to see working with a coach not as a stigma but rather as a sign of the organization's interest in supporting executives' successful careers. This shift benefits both the executive and the organization.

Supporting Your Transition Needs

Sometimes, sponsors will seek coaching for executives who are considered high performers and who are either preparing to move into roles where different skills are needed or simply seeking to strengthen their edge in current roles. Sponsors may seek to groom executives for senior roles or, as it is often put, help them become more polished or more strategic. Or executives may be moving laterally to new functions or organizations with different cultures or prevailing leadership styles. Typical development issues for executives in transition include strengthening leadership presence, building relationships with senior leaders, leading others who have more technical expertise, and influencing others.

Strengthening leadership presence. Ed Romaine was a popular manager who led through consensus building. His bosses wondered whether, if promoted, he would be able to play a strong role in representing his own group's interests, not just in facilitating consensus among others.

Building relationships with senior leaders. Suzanne Jacobs was beloved by her midlevel clients within the organization because she got things done. However, she was promoted to a role in which she was expected to build relationships at senior levels. She needed to both understand these senior leaders' perspective on organizational direction and get their support for her team's proposed initiatives. She had to learn to connect with them by focusing on what they cared about.

Leading others with more technical expertise. Peter McCall was promoted to lead a larger group, and it was the first time he was not more technically proficient than those who worked for him. He had to learn to lead without relying primarily on his technical expertise.

Influencing others. Jamie Grady was considered a high-potential manager. The managers whose area he supported saw him as very effective, because he invariably completed their requests. However, he wished to change his relationship with them to one in which he could actually influence them to adopt initiatives that would help to achieve their goals—rather than simply respond to their requests.

Often coaching during a role transition focuses on helping executives understand new expectations, expand perspective about their roles, develop new skills, and understand how to manage strengths and limitations in the new role. The transition is generally a low-risk, high-reward coaching opportunity. If there is a common risk, it is the relationship patterns and perceptions of others who continue to see the executive in old ways, as the relatively more junior person he or she has been. For this reason, transition coaching needs to focus strongly on helping others' perceptions evolve.

Enhancing Your Strategic Effectiveness

Sometimes, leaders of a group may choose to sponsor coaching for all members of their leadership team. This effort may be in response to a mandated shift in the group's purpose or strategy, or because of challenges to the group's effectiveness. For example, leaders may seek to increase the value their team delivers to customers or to improve the team's internal alignment and collaboration.

Increasing value delivered to customers. Sid Galinsky, the head of a corporate information technology group, had a vision that his group should be more than a technology provider; he wanted to be a strategic partner with the business his group supported. He sought coaching for his leaders to help them develop their style and approach in a way that supported this vision. In addition, he participated in coaching himself, to help him lead the change in his group.

Improving internal alignment of team. Rosanne Sciorra, the head of a corporate research group, wanted to help her direct reports address their unique leadership development issues and learn how to work more collectively and less as functional "silos."

In situations such as these, training and other interventions at the group level can supplement individual coaching by giving executives a common picture of purpose, operating principles, needed skills, and objectives. The most common risk in this situation is that the team's leader, who typically initiates such a coaching process, may initially want the team developed without seeing his or her own development as a necessary part of the solution. For this reason, coaches who work with a team must contract explicitly with the team's leader to ensure his or her willingness to participate in coaching and development with the others.

To summarize, if you are thinking about coaching in any of these three situations, you may be on the right track. However, to optimize coaching effectiveness, you must address two areas that are just as critical: your readiness to be coached and the willingness of key colleagues to engage in the process.

YOUR READINESS TO BE COACHED

If coaching is to have a positive impact, your participation must be voluntary and you must involve yourself in the process in several ways. The coach should discuss these issues with you during the initial contracting meeting (see Chapter 5), but it is worth anticipating these expectations even before a coach enters the picture.

Believing That You Can Benefit from Participating

You must acknowledge that you struggle with certain leadership issues and that you could be more effective in these areas with the help of new insights and tools. This acknowledgment is more than simply an interest in learning new skills. It also means recognizing that you, like any executive, have a personal leadership style related to your character, and that this style includes inherent strengths and limitations that must be managed. If you are extremely defensive and feel that all the issues perceived by colleagues are someone else's fault or if you are unwilling to look at your own contribution to the problems you are experiencing, then coaching effectiveness will be severely limited.

It is quite common and appropriate for you to have a different perspective on your performance issues from that of your boss or sponsor. For example, you may emphasize the impact that outside forces, such as other people or the business situation, have on your problems. If you have this view, you can still be a good coaching candidate, as long as you acknowledge that your own behavior has also contributed to the situation. In fact, a gap between your sponsor's perceptions and how you view a situation can provide other powerful motives for you to engage. You could see the coaching process as an opportunity to close the gap and influence how your sponsor evaluates your leadership effectiveness. If there is such a gap, a coach should align your expectations for your performance and development with your sponsor's and ensure that the sponsor and others are willing to change their behavior and perceptions.

Being Willing to Devote a Certain Amount of Time to Coaching and to Give It Priority

Coaching-related activities typically take up approximately one day every month. You must agree to attend scheduled coaching meetings, even when other commitments are pressing. There are always other urgent matters, but stressful times are among the most useful coaching opportunities. You must also agree to contact the coach for implementation support in relevant situations, such as times when you need to think through and plan important meetings or conversations.

Being Willing to Ask for and Accept Feedback

The coach typically begins the process by interviewing colleagues to provide confidential input on your behavior and its effects. Later, you will be expected to ask for and receive feedback directly from colleagues.

Being Willing to Test and Revise Your Assumptions About Your Development Needs

Some executives, in their initial meeting with a potential coach, describe what they have concluded about their development issues and offer solutions. For example, one executive said in a contracting meeting, "I just need some tools and techniques for leading a larger group." The problem is that you may be out of touch with how others perceive your behavior—or you may be afraid to look more deeply.

Being Willing to Practice New Behaviors

Your new behaviors will not come naturally, and this struggle may be frustrating. Eventually, you must go public with your desire to grow and change and accept the increased vulnerability that can go along with this step. As we've discussed, some executives worry that others may lose respect for them or not want to follow their leadership if they show their weakness by saying that they are trying to change or learn. If you are not willing to rethink this assumption, it will be a barrier to participating in important coaching activities and, most likely, an insurmountable barrier to change.

CHECKLIST 1

Assessing Your
Readiness for Coaching

Positive Factors (the more of these, the higher the readiness)

☐ Do you acknowledge that your effectiveness could improve through dealing with the inherent limitations of your style?

☐ Are you willing to devote time and priority to coaching activities, even when tempted by other urgent matters?

☐ Are you willing to ask colleagues for feedback on your behavior and impact?

☐ Are you willing to try new behaviors, even if you initially struggle with them?

☐ Are you willing to show others your interest in changing, even if this step makes you feel anxious?

☐ Are you prepared to share authentic needs, feelings, and concerns with a coach?

Negative Factors (the more of these, the lower the readiness)

☐ Do you blame all your challenges on others or on situations?

☐ Are you convinced that you already know what you need to do to become more effective?

☐ Do you believe that you have few, if any, behaviors that need improvement?

☐ Do you believe that your ideas and approaches usually lead to the best solution?

Being Willing to Be Authentic with a Coach

Granted, you will have to find a coach who will honor basic guidelines of confidentiality and make you feel comfortable. But once a coaching relationship has begun, the coach's ability to help will be affected by your willingness to share thoughts, feelings, reactions, concerns, and wishes.

You may find Checklist 1 helpful in determining your readiness for coaching.

However, the pressure to change should not rest solely on you. If your colleagues have this expectation, then the impact of coaching will be drastically limited. Therefore, let's take a look at the changes others must be willing to make.

COLLEAGUES' WILLINGNESS TO ENGAGE

You are embedded in a web of perceptions and relationships at work. How others see you, and how they interpret your behavior, can affect their reactions and your effectiveness. Your colleagues, then, must also engage in the coaching process by questioning their own attitudes and behavior in relation to you, as follows.

Being Honest with Themselves About Whether They Have Already Passed Judgment on You

Many sponsors turn to a coach only after they are frustrated with their own efforts to develop an executive. If they already have judged you, then coaching you in isolation will almost never change how they feel about you. If other people have accumulated years of frustrations concerning you, then the coaching process will need to include mutual work to repair relationships, and others will need to recognize their part in improving those relationships.

Being Clear About How Much Change They Expect to See

Leadership style is not like a coat you can change at will but rather is rooted in your basic character. You can become more aware of your own behavior patterns, increase sensitivity to the dynamics in any situation, and make better choices at each moment, but you will not become a totally different person. If sponsors are looking for you to adopt a completely different style, they will end up disappointed. If, in contrast, sponsors are looking for you to become a more mature, skilled, and effective version of your current self, then their expectations are more realistic.

Being Willing to Accept That Their Initial Judgments of You Are Not Complete

Sponsors, especially senior ones, often incorrectly assume that they have all the relevant information about your style and development needs, when in fact they are seeing only one side of you. Meanwhile, different people in your life—peers, reports, family—are seeing different sides. Relying on only sponsors' diagnoses will lead to incomplete solutions, and sponsors must accept this.

Coaching, ideally, is like peeling an onion: not only your layers should be exposed, but also those representing the perceptions of the people around you. Often sponsors begin a coaching effort by labeling a particular issue or individual as the problem. Over time, though, they come to understand that many factors contribute to the situation, including others' behaviors, the organizational culture, and performance expectations. For example, Douglas Chen was criticized by many colleagues for being inattentive to detail and overly reliant on intuition for making decisions. These colleagues came to realize, over the course of Chen's coaching process, that their culture was so focused on data that they lacked an overall vision and, in fact, needed someone with a complementary approach. They realized this because they were willing to get underneath their initial perceptions and assumptions and redefine the problem and solution based on a deeper understanding.

Being Willing to Look at Their Own Contributions and to Change Their Own Behaviors

For example, your manager may have been avoiding giving you direct feedback. Or team members who have complained that you are autocratic may have behaved passively when given the opportunity to participate. You can change your own behavior, but results and relationships may not improve unless all parties address their contributions to the situation.

Being Willing to Give You Ongoing Feedback

Coaches frequently discover during their initial meetings with potential clients that sponsors have never given the executives in question direct and specific feedback about their behavior and its impact, or discussed any expectations for change. If development is to be sustained, sponsors (and others) must change their habits and start giving feedback directly to you. This change is critical but often difficult to accomplish. When executives ask for feedback, colleagues will often avoid specific and candid remarks and instead offer empty phrases, such as "You did a good job." Away from the executives, though, they may discuss their true reactions in detail with other colleagues or with coaches. Your colleagues must learn to share this feedback directly with you.

Being Willing to Alter Their Judgments and to See You Differently

Often, as executives are trying to change their behavior, others will observe them through selective lenses. They may focus on the behaviors that are consistent with their old judgments and ignore new or positive behaviors. Or they may see a behavior and infer an underlying intent that is consistent with their old judgments. It is critical that colleagues be aware of this tendency, test their interpretations of your behavior with you, and look not only for the persistent old behaviors but also for evidence of the desired new behaviors.

Checklist 2 summarizes the key dimensions on which to assess colleagues' willingness to participate. You can use this to assess situations or, better yet, raise and discuss these issues directly with your colleagues.

The other critical ingredient for success of a coaching engagement is the coach you choose. I'll discuss that choice in the next chapter.

CHECKLIST 2

Assessing Colleagues'
Willingness to Participate

Positive Factors (the more of these, the higher the willingness)

☐ Do your colleagues expect you to broaden your perspective and increase your skills and effectiveness but understand that you will keep your same basic style?

☐ Are they willing to modify their initial definition of your development needs and other contributing factors?

☐ Are they willing to look at their own contribution to problems and develop their own behavior to support change?

☐ Are they willing to give you ongoing feedback on important behaviors?

☐ Are they willing to change their habitual interpretations of your behavior and motives?

Negative Factors (the more of these, the lower the willingness)

☐ Have they already passed judgment on you?

☐ Do they expect the coach to accept their definition of the problem and/or solution?

☐ Do they expect you to adopt a totally different style from your current one?

☐ Do they expect an overnight change in your style?

☐ Do they expect only progressive improvement, with no backsliding or side steps?

SUMMARY

Three Factors Affecting the Likelihood of Success of Coaching

EXECUTIVE'S DEVELOPMENT NEEDS		
Type of Need	Potential Benefits from Coaching	Potential Risks of Coaching
Performance • Interpersonal abrasiveness • Micromanagement • Customer dissatisfaction	• Potential to preserve organization's investment in a valuable executive • Getting executive to see costs of behavior that may have been rewarded in the past	• Resistance of executive • Ingrained perceptions of others • Large gap between colleagues' expectations and executive's capability
Transition needs • Leadership presence • Relationships with senior leaders • Leadership of others with more technical expertise • Influence	• Understanding of expectations of new role • Understanding of how best to use strengths and limitations in new role	• Colleagues' tendency to continue seeing executive as more junior
Strategic effectiveness • Value to customer • Internal team alignment	• Ability to address effectiveness of a whole team as well as individual effectiveness	• Team leaders' reluctance to see their own need for development

SUMMARY cont'd

EXECUTIVE'S READINESS FOR CHANGE	COLLEAGUES' WILLINGNESS TO ENGAGE
• Belief in potential benefit from participating • Willingness to devote time and give priority to the process • Willingness to ask for and accept feedback • Willingness to test and revise assumptions about own developmental needs • Willingness to practice new behaviors • Willingness to be authentic with a coach	• Honesty about whether they have already passed judgment on the executive • Clarity about how much change they expect to see • Willingness to accept that their initial judgments of executive may not be accurate • Willingness to look at own contributions and to change own behavior • Willingness to give executive ongoing feedback • Willingness to test assumptions and see executive differently

4

How to Choose a Coach

Key Capabilities to Assess

Once you are ready to enter into a coaching engagement, you will need to choose your coach. Many executives jump into this selection process without considering what they need; they pick a coach based on referrals from colleagues or hire the first one they interview. Or sponsors will send a few coaches for interviews and ask the executive to select one based on how the coach "fits." As the client, you should do the choosing, of course, but you might find it helpful to have a few pointers so you know what to look for. This chapter discusses the key aspects of the coaching role and gives you tools for assessing potential coaches, so that you can collect the information you need to make a good match.

COACHING COMPETENCIES

During the first meeting with a potential coach, you will need to assess the person's ability to guide you. A coach should be able to balance support and challenge; help you create feedback loops; assist you in clarifying your purpose, values, and interests; structure the development process; broaden your perspective; teach concepts and skills; maintain confidentiality; and influence others' views of you.

Balancing Support and Challenge

It is difficult even in the best of situations for most executives to show (or even experience) uncertainty, express fear, or ask for help. However, for development to occur, it's critical that you do these very things, and you are more likely to do so if your coach can create a safe environment. Coaches do this in part by showing that they "get" you—that they listen to you and understand and respect your interests, values, and concerns. Such understanding enables you to feel accepted, be open about your true thoughts and feelings, and be willing to try new behaviors. This openness then enables the coach to help you focus on reaching your goals and addressing your true concerns. The more subtle effect of this acceptance is that you realize that it is okay to be your authentic self, and this realization can help you stop taking ineffective actions that are driven by your desire to appear perfect.

On the other side of this balancing act, the coach must be more than just a cheerleader. He or she must also provide challenges to propel you beyond your habitual behaviors and perceptions. He or she must confront you, directly and nonjudgmentally, with the impact of your actions and must probe the motives and assumptions underlying your behavior. The coach must be willing to push you out of your comfort zone because there is a level of learning about yourself that can be reached only with some discomfort.

One tool a coach can use to challenge you and help build your awareness is his or her personal experience with you. The way you treat your coach reflects the way you treat others in the organization, although the significance of your behavior will depend on how you perceive the coach: Do you see the coach as a subordinate (because he or she is not part of the hierarchy), as a vendor (because he or she is an external consultant), or as an authority figure (because he or she has a relationship with your boss)? Do gender, race, or other personal characteristics influence the way you interact with the coach?

Regardless of any of these factors, an effective coach should have the insight and the skill to give you feedback on behavior that is relevant to your goals. George Watts, for example, had received feedback that he was insensitive to others' needs. Addressing this was one of the goals of his coaching project. While working with his coach, Watts repeatedly canceled meetings with her without warning, including meetings she had specifically traveled to attend, and then failed to even acknowledge the cancellation when they next saw each other. This was relevant feedback for the coach to share with Watts. Together they probed (without judgment) what Watts was thinking, or not thinking, when he decided to schedule another appointment during his regular coaching meeting time, or when he chose not to inform the coach. This helped Watts become more aware of how he was behaving similarly with his colleagues. Coaches must have the emotional competence to separate themselves from their role if they are to raise such issues impartially for the purpose of learning. They also must have the capacity to be authentic, to be straight with you about their observations and their reactions to you.

Helping You Create Feedback Loops

Initially, coaches must serve as the conduit for feedback from colleagues because others rarely share authentic feedback with executives. They must solicit information from colleagues in a way that satisfies their need for confidentiality and manage any anxiety they might have about divulging information they consider risky. This requirement means establishing clear agreements about how the information will be used or if respondents will be identified—and never losing sight of those boundaries.

The coach should help you build skills to create relationships in which you can ask for feedback directly on an ongoing basis. A good coach will not seek dependence from you but rather will want to teach you how to manage your development in the future. The coach can help form links with colleagues—possibly beginning with the initial assessment interviews—and also teach others how to frame useful feedback. For example, the coach can help colleagues distinguish between a specific description of behavior (which is useful) and a vague judgment (which is not). The coach will also help you plan how you will ask colleagues for feedback, and how you will manage the ensuing conversation in a way that's not defensive. Finally, the coach can help you learn how to make sense of the feedback you receive by deciding what is relevant and valid, which issues to address, and how best to address them.

Assisting You in Clarifying Your Purpose, Values, and Interests

The coach's role in this important goal is to help you articulate your core purpose, values, and interests by clarifying both your development goals and your career and life goals. The coach should also help you learn how to decipher your interests—your wants, needs, concerns, and boundaries—in any particular situation. Once you become more comfortable identifying your purpose, values, and interests, your coach can then help you act more consistently with them.

Structuring the Development Process

To support your development of desired behaviors, the coach must help you manage each step of the coaching project: establishing a contract, getting input from others, reviewing feedback and planning development, holding regular coaching meetings to practice new behaviors, implementing those behaviors in your daily work, and assessing results. The coach should provide you with a clear road map for how the process will work and then help keep the process moving over time, especially when you are apt to let it slide because of urgent work matters or your natural resistance to change.

Broadening Your Perspective

The coach is there not to give advice or to make decisions but to broaden your perspective by helping you first understand and then break free of the limits of your own perspective. A perspective shift may be the most significant factor in helping executives change behavior and results. A perspective shift will change your assumptions, expand the information you find useful, alter how you perform key skills, and enhance your ability to create organizational value. The coach can broaden perspective by providing additional viewpoints, helping you look at situations as others might, asking new questions, and offering new approaches, all with an understanding of your current perspective, strengths, and limitations.

Teaching Concepts and Skills

Often, executives are so immersed in the world of action that they never develop a clear understanding of their role. If this is true of you, you may believe that you must deal directly with every issue that crosses your desk. Your coach can help you step back and get a clearer picture of what is and is not a part of your role.

In addition, the coach should have a mental model of what leadership means, what it takes to be effective, and what key skills are required. For example, in our firm, leadership is geared toward getting shared commitment from a group of people to achieve a common purpose. Key skills include collaboration, expectation management, influencing, conflict resolution, and developing others. Your coach should be able to teach skills relevant to your situation and then help you implement them in your daily interactions.

Maintaining Confidentiality

To be effective, the coach must maintain relationships based on trust. During a project, coaches come into possession of a great deal of sensitive and confidential information. Also, they may be working with several different members of the same organization, or even members of the same team. Coaches must be able to maintain boundaries and keep information confidential. If they wish to share information from clients or colleagues, they must first get consent.

Influencing Others' Views of You

It is not enough for a coach to help you change your behavior; he or she must also help others see that change. To do so, the coach will have to engage with your colleagues to help them see the issues more broadly, to get them involved in your development, and possibly to help them change their behavior in relation to you. He or she should be discussing colleagues' perceptions, judgments, and expectations of you and testing their willingness to adopt broader views. The coach is likely to share with you what he or she learns in these conversations and should be explicit about the fact that he or she is doing so.

You can expect your coach to influence others' views by

- Coaching your relationships, not just you
- Challenging, and helping others challenge, initial assumptions that the entire problem resides with you
  - Encouraging them to consider structural and situational contributions
  - Helping them consider their personal contributions
- Contracting with key colleagues
  - Determining their desired outcomes of the process
  - Assessing their willingness to share feedback
  - Asking them to participate in conversations about new mutual expectations
- Facilitating conversations between you and colleagues
  - Enabling you to share coaching insights and development plans
  - Negotiating new expectations in both directions

- Helping you solicit ongoing feedback from colleagues on relevant behaviors

If your coach does not raise these points with you in your initial conversations, you should make sure that they will be included in the coaching process.

ROLES THE COACH SHOULD NOT PLAY

There are several roles that are not appropriate for coaches because they do not build your capability for independent action. Although some of these roles may be common and alluring traps, effective coaches should never succumb to them.

- **Cheerleader.** Coaches should not be on the sidelines, telling you that everything you do is great.

- **Therapist.** Executive coaches are not supposed to help you strictly with your personal adjustment and psychological issues, independent of your performance in the organization and of others' expectations.

- **Executor of the boss's wishes.** Coaches should do more than just force you to conform to others' expectations.

- **Shadow manager.** Coaches cannot advise you on business decisions or step in and act on your behalf.

- **One-sided advocate.** Coaches need to look at all viewpoints and not just take the side of either you or your colleagues.

RELATED SELECTION ISSUES

Two other issues people frequently mention when selecting a coach are "fit" and credentials. Both are loaded and complex notions that need to be fleshed out.

The Issue of "Fit"

In your first meeting with a potential coach, you will get a lot of information. Coaches should share information about themselves, their philosophy of coaching, and their personal style. If you meet with more than one potential coach, you will discover that each individual coach's style is unique. For example, my partner is more directive and structured than I am, and some people prefer his style, but others prefer mine.

However, you must make sure to balance the issue of fit against your need for support and challenge. Fit must encompass more than simply liking the coach. It must include believing that this coach can help you change.

The Question of Credentials

The field of executive coaching is not one associated with well-trod traditional career paths or specific educational backgrounds. Most coaches come to the practice after a gradual evolution from roles in related areas. For example, coaches could come from internal human resources departments and specialize in leadership development or organizational effectiveness, or from careers in external consulting in organizational change or leadership training. Some individuals come to coaching from careers in counseling or therapy. Many, but not all, coaches have advanced degrees in related areas such as business, psychology, or organizational behavior.

What really matters is that through education, work experience, and continued training, coaches understand both individual and organizational dynamics. Each area of expertise is necessary but insufficient on its own. It's impossible to help people change ingrained behaviors without understanding the dynamics of individual personality and how people develop. Coaching is not therapy, but clinical insight and perspective are useful. At the same time, it's also important that coaches have some understanding of how organizations work, what kinds of outcomes will be valued from colleagues' perspectives, and how executives' demands from networks of working relationships and different roles will affect development.

We've discussed all the preliminary issues in embarking on a coaching process: how coaching can help lead to successful development, whether coaching can help you in your particular situation, and how you can choose the right coach for you. Once you've worked through these issues, you are ready to begin a coaching relationship with someone. The next section helps you through the stages in that relationship by telling you what to expect and how you can best participate in each stage.

SUMMARY

Key Dimensions for Assessing a Potential Coach

COACHING COMPETENCY	COACH'S CONDUCT TO LOOK FOR
Balancing support and challenge	• Understands your goals and values without judging you • Paraphrases your statements in a way that evidences such understanding • Shows willingness to challenge you on your counterproductive behaviors and attitudes
Helping you create feedback loops	• Plans to help you have conversations with colleagues to discuss their perceptions of you and get their support for your development
Helping you clarify purpose, values, and interests	• Inquires about your personal purpose and values • Helps you make choices based on your key interests

Structuring the development process	• Gives you a clear road map of the steps in the process:
	  – Contracting
	  – Feedback
	  – Development planning
	  – Implementation
	  – Assessment

SUMMARY cont'd

COACHING COMPETENCY	COACH'S CONDUCT TO LOOK FOR
Broadening your perspective	• Offers you new ways of seeing the situations and challenges you described
Teaching concepts and skills	• Provides examples of skills and models to teach you • Links examples to your day-to-day work and helps you implement them in real work settings
Maintaining confidentiality	• Describes how he or she will handle confidentiality (yours and others')
Reframing others' definitions of the situation	• Is willing to engage with co-workers and address their perceptions and contributions
"Fitting" with you	• Makes you feel that his or her style will complement yours • Makes you feel comfortable or, if you are uncomfortable, makes you feel that you have something to learn by confronting your discomfort
Having credentials	• Explains how his or her background (career and education) will contribute to the process – Understands individual development – Understands organizational dynamics

Part Three

MANAGING THE
COACHING PROCESS

5

Contracting

Agreement on How and Why to Proceed

After you have decided to embark on a coaching engagement and have chosen a coach, the next step is to work with your coach to decide what to do—a process called *contracting*. This chapter explains the objectives, key activities, and output of the contracting phase.

OBJECTIVES

The contracting phase is intended to accomplish several objectives:

- Help you and your coach begin forming a relationship
- Give you a complete understanding of how the process will work
- Establish desired outcomes of coaching, from your perspective and from the perspective of the sponsor (these outcomes may be different)
- Clarify roles and expectations of all key participants: the coach, you, and the sponsor
- Test the commitment of key participants

KEY ACTIVITIES

In the contracting phase, your coach will meet with your sponsor, with you, and then (optional but preferable) with you and your sponsor together. These meetings, and the information exchanged in them, will enable the coach to assess the appropriateness of the project, as well as help everyone involved commit to the process and reach a mutual agreement about goals and steps, respective roles, and ways the process will be tailored to address specific needs.

Coach's Meeting with the Sponsor

The coaching process must include the people whose interests and expectations influence your ability to be successful and effective. It's critical for the coach to meet with the sponsor for several reasons.

Identifying the sponsor's goals for coaching. The coach will want to clarify the sponsor's goals for this coaching process, including any concerns he or she may have about your current performance. The coach will learn what outcomes the sponsor requires to deem the project a success. This meeting will also help the coach prepare the sponsor to notice the desired changes in you.

Describing the coaching process. The coach will explain the assumptions, objectives, and steps of the coaching process, as well as the responsibilities of each party. The coach has allegiance to two people—you and the sponsor—and must balance the sponsor's interests (improved capability and performance) and your interests (trust and support for your development) if the process is to work effectively.

The coach makes a commitment to provide certain support for the sponsor, including regular meetings to discuss progress. However, the coach also has a commitment to maintain confidentiality in the coaching relationship. Usually, this balance is accomplished through the steps listed below. You own all information generated about your behavior and style, and your coach may not divulge it to anyone else, including the sponsor. The coach will facilitate meetings between you and the sponsor to share feedback, and you will choose what to share in those meetings.

In this meeting, sponsor and coach will also discuss the fee and other terms such as expenses and length of contract, and ensure that the sponsor agrees to these terms.

Establishing the sponsor's role. The coach will ask the sponsor to commit to certain activities.

- Meet with you and share his or her goals for the process
- Participate in a preliminary interview with the coach to provide feedback about your leadership
- Review your insights and development plan with you
- Share ongoing and timely feedback with you about relevant behaviors
- Be open to changing any preexisting judgments about you
- Meet with you (and possibly the coach) periodically to review progress
- Meet with you (and possibly the coach) at the end of the coaching contract to assess goal achievement, determine future development needs, and discuss continuing support

Testing the sponsor's willingness to proceed. The sponsor is now in a position to give informed consent to the process.

Sample 1 provides a typical agenda for the meeting between the coach and sponsor. Although the specific agenda will vary according to your coach's style and preferences, these general topics should be addressed.

SAMPLE 1

Coach's Agenda for Entry Meeting with Sponsor

- Review coaching process and test for sponsor's reactions or concerns
  - List objectives
  - Explain steps
  - Set terms

- Review information about coach and address questions

- Clarify sponsor's goals for executive's development

- Discuss expectations for sponsor's role
  - Participate in an interview
  - Hold periodic meetings to review development plans and progress
  - Give executive ongoing feedback
  - Be willing to modify judgments about the executive

- Test readiness to commit

- Prepare for next steps
  - Plan three-way contracting meeting with executive
  - Schedule interview

Coach's Meeting with You

By the time you meet with a potential coach, the sponsor most likely will have already discussed the coaching project with you, and you will have indicated willingness to participate in the process. The coach should not consider the project approved until after this meeting with you, regardless of the sponsor's position.

Identifying your goals for coaching. The coach will want to learn about you and probably will ask you questions about such topics as what you see as the major challenges of your role, what outcomes you would like to see from the coaching process, and what insight you have into your current leadership style, strengths, and limitations.

Describing the coaching process. As in the coach's meeting with the sponsor, the coach will clarify the assumptions, objectives, and steps of the coaching process, as well as the scope and boundaries of confidentiality.

Discussing expectations of you. The coach will probably ask you to allocate specific times to meet with him or her and to implement agreed-on actions and tasks. The coach will also likely ask you to be willing to try new behaviors and challenge your existing assumptions and beliefs.

Testing your willingness to proceed. It is critical that you give your informed consent to continue with the coaching process.

Planning next steps. If you are willing to continue with the process, the contracting meeting may also be a time to discuss the initial steps of scheduling coaching meetings and collecting data. If interviews are planned, the coach may wish to discuss potential interviewees with you and ask that you contact them to request their participation.

How much information should you divulge in this meeting? For example, some executives who are referred for coaching are not entirely satisfied in their current position (or organization) and are thinking about making a change. If you are in a situation like this, you may not want your boss or other organization members to learn about your concerns. However, this is certainly information that's relevant to the coaching process, and your coach can potentially help you with the decision. (It would be prudent to confirm your coach's commitment to confidentiality before you discuss this.) Most coaches won't see the situation as a conflict; rather, they will see it as helping both you and your organization make a good choice, even if this choice involves you leaving the organization. A good coach will challenge you to identify how you

SAMPLE 2

Coach's Agenda for Entry Meeting with Executive

- Review coaching process and test for executive's reactions or concerns
  - Objectives of coaching process
    - Increase effectiveness
    - Develop self-awareness
    - Broaden perspective
    - Acquire new skills
    - Clarify purpose
    - Focus on stuck areas

  - Steps in coaching process
    - Assess leadership
      - Assess behavior through interviews
      - Assess style through instruments
    - Go over feedback
    - Design development plan
    - Coach through implementation

- Share information about coach's background, philosophy, and style

- Ask for executive's interests in development
  - Current situation, role, and challenges
  - Self-perceptions of strengths, limitations, and style
  - Goals for coaching

- Test executive's readiness to commit

- Prepare for next steps
  - Data collection
  - Three-way contracting meeting with sponsor
  - Scheduling coaching meetings

are contributing to the frustration you're experiencing and help you use your current situation as an opportunity to develop yourself and change things for the better. Otherwise, you're likely to repeat your behavior in your next job and the same problems might arise.

Sample 2 provides a typical agenda for the meeting between you and your coach. Again, although your specific meeting might not take this exact form, these general issues should be covered.

Coach's Meeting with You and Your Sponsor Together

This meeting is optional but can be beneficial in getting your respective interests and expectations on the table. This meeting might occur before the coach meets with you alone, or it might replace the meeting between the coach and sponsor. If such a meeting is held, it typically includes the following activities.

Discussing the sponsor's and your goals for coaching. This meeting provides an excellent opportunity to hear how your sponsor perceives your leadership strengths and limitations and your development needs and share how you see these. The coach can help by asking questions if either of you is vague or indirect.

Clarifying the process. The coach will explain the basic steps and flow of the coaching process and answer any questions you or the sponsor may have about how it will work.

Sharing interests and concerns about the process. This conversation can provide the setting for an open conversation about what you and the sponsor want to have happen as a result of coaching, what you do not want to have happen, and any concerns either of you may have.

Agreeing on desired outcomes for the process and how success will be measured. Your goals may differ somewhat from those of your sponsor, and you may have some goals you don't wish to divulge to your sponsor. Most coaches will accept and work with this reality, as long as you understand your sponsor's goals and as long as you and the sponsor agree on some shared outcomes and measures.

Agreeing on roles and expectations. Ideally, you will walk out of this conversation with a shared picture of all the parties' roles in the process and a clear understanding of what each of you expects.

Assessing the Appropriateness of the Coaching Project

Not only must you and the sponsor give informed consent to the process, but the coach must decide whether the conditions are right for a successful project. An ethical coach will not take on a project without carefully considering important conditions that can affect its success.

Determining your commitment to doing the work of behavior change. Some prospective clients will declare strong commitment to the sponsor because they feel compelled to, but present a different picture to the coach. Or they will indicate a willingness to participate as long as it does not require too much time or effort. In such situations, the coach must use good judgment to determine whether these variables will jeopardize the project.

Determining the sponsor's commitment to doing the work of changing relevant perceptions and behaviors. Similarly, some sponsors will show more enthusiasm about your potential for success when you are present than when they are speaking with the coach privately. Or they will show enthusiasm for the process, but not for the idea that they may have to participate, and maybe even change their behavior, to support your development. Often sponsors will identify a problem performer without acknowledging their own and others' contributions to the situation. The coach must attempt to assess whether sponsors are willing to address those contributions, which will affect whether any effort you make to change has a chance to succeed. Again, the coach must use good judgment and be willing to directly confront the sponsor's behavior.

OUTPUT

The tangible output of the contracting phase is two written documents (one for you, one for the sponsor) summarizing the agreements made in the meetings. This document typically includes the following:

- General goals of a coaching project
- Specific goals of this coaching project
  - Yours
  - Sponsor's
- Key activities
  - Description
  - Purpose
  - Timing and duration
- Expectations of key parties
  - Yours
  - Sponsor's
  - Coach's
- Confidentiality
  - Ownership of feedback materials
  - Anonymity of responses
  - Confidentiality of your conversations with the coach
  - Expectations that you will share development information

- Terms (usually sent only to sponsor)
  - Fees and expenses
- Expected results
- Next steps

Although the contracts written for sponsors are similar to those for executives in most respects, there may be slight differences. Both will address overall project goals, steps to take, and confidentiality matters. Your contract will likely go into more detail in areas most relevant to you, such as your goals for the process (some of which may have been shared with the coach in confidence), next steps in the coaching process, and expectations of your participation in the project. The sponsor's contract will include more detail in areas that are most relevant to him or her—for example, the financial terms and conditions and expectations of the sponsor's participation in the process.

The contract is important not just because it documents agreements, but because it ensures that the coach's picture of coaching activities, objectives, terms, and so on is shared by both you and your sponsor. Revisions can also be made at this time. Samples 3 and 4 provide sample contracts for the executive and sponsor.

There is also an intangible output of the contracting phase: a shared understanding among you, your coach, and the sponsor about the goals of your development, as well as a new relationship that will move you through the process.

As soon as you have completed this phase, your coach will probably want to begin collecting information about your leadership— information that will be shared with you and used to construct a development plan. The coach may also begin having coaching meetings with you even before receiving feedback, based on what he or she already knows about your style and development interests. This isn't a universal practice, but I believe it is desirable, because you can immediately begin increasing your self-awareness and trying new behaviors.

Contract, Executive's Version

Date

George Watts

Dear George,

The following is a proposal for your personal coaching project and summarizes goals, coaching interests, key activities, confidentiality, and next steps.

Goals

This process is intended to accomplish the following general goals:

- Give you a clear understanding of your leadership behavior, style, and impact, focusing on your core strengths, limitations, and development needs
- Identify challenges in your current and emerging roles and explore possible gaps between your skills and those challenges
- Identify areas in which to focus your development over the next year to increase your effectiveness
- Implement this plan by developing specific behaviors in critical situations and relationships

Coaching Interests

In our initial contracting meeting, you described your current situation. Sometime next year, you expect to take over the leadership of your group. You have progressed far in management at a relatively young age. Given the intensified leadership challenges you expect to face, you identified three key interests for development.

First, you wish to address issues in your interpersonal style. Although you have extensive knowledge and strong capabilities in terms of strategic judgment and problem solving, you have received feedback that your style of working with others can create tensions. You tend to be overly directive with reports, and you can become frustrated when expected to collaborate with peers. As a result, those relationships tend to be less positive than your relationships with superiors.

Second, you wish to identify and strengthen key relationships. This will involve identifying which individuals are critical for achieving your goals and building strong reciprocal relationships with them.

Third, you described feeling increasingly divided between the person you are at work and the person you are at home, finding it difficult to act consistently with your personal values. As work demands increase, it will be helpful to explore ways of integrating both selves more closely.

Key Activities
The following is an outline of the key activities in the coaching process, including purpose, actions, and timing.

Contract for Desired Outcomes
Purpose
The purpose of this activity is to define key development issues for this process, including input from both you and your boss.

Actions
- An initial meeting between the two of us to identify your interests
- A second meeting between you, your boss, and me to hear his interests

Timing
Completed as soon as possible after the agreement is signed

Ongoing Coaching
Purpose
The purpose of this activity is to guide your behavior change, support implementation of your action plans, assess impact, and adapt strategies for change.

Actions
Ongoing coaching may involve observation, facilitation of meetings, skill training, and coaching conversations to prepare and debrief your actions. We may also develop customized methods for you to assess your own progress with key stakeholders. These activities are likely to require about one day per month, spread across multiple meetings and conversations.

Timing
Completed continually throughout the contract period

Assess Your Behavior and Its Effects
Purpose
The purpose of this activity is to develop a picture of how you and others perceive your behavior, its impact on others, and its effect on organization performance. We also will seek to understand how your fundamental style shapes your behavior.

Actions
- I will interview you and selected colleagues you identify.
- You will complete several instruments and a background information form.

Timing
Completed approximately ten weeks after the agreement is signed

Jointly Interpret Assessment Results
Purpose
The purpose of this activity is to understand your current leadership approach, including strengths, limitations, biases, and patterns. This understanding is fundamental to the creation of a personal development plan and also helps guide the coaching conversations during implementation.

Actions
A one-day feedback meeting, preferably away from the workplace

Timing
Completed approximately twelve weeks after the agreement is signed

Create a Personal Development Plan
Purpose
The purpose of this activity is to select behaviors that you want to change and then identify potential measures. The selection of specific behaviors is guided by your coaching interests, your boss's interests, and the information that emerges from the feedback.

Actions
A half-day consolidation and planning meeting

Timing
Completed approximately two weeks after the feedback meeting

Conduct Feedback Meetings
Purpose
The purpose of these meetings is to involve colleagues in your development effort, including your boss, key clients, and others you want to influence. This step gives you feedback about your change effort and enables others to see the results of your development.

Actions
Several very brief meetings to review your summary feedback and development plans with your boss and selected colleagues

Timing
Completed within one month after your planning session

Midcourse Review Meeting
Purpose
The purpose of this meeting is to test progress and to redirect coaching actions, if necessary.

Actions
• A meeting between the two of us to discuss progress and issues
• A second meeting between you, your boss, and me to hear his observations and suggestions

Timing
Completed approximately six months after the contract is signed

Final Assessment Meeting
Purpose
The purpose of this meeting is to test progress, evaluate the coaching process, and identify subsequent development goals to share with your boss.

Actions

- An initial meeting between the two of us to test progress against established measures
- A second meeting between you, your boss, and me to share these evaluations and hear his observations and reactions

Timing
Completed approximately twelve months after the contract is signed, with the option of a one-time six-month coaching extension

Confidentiality
All information generated during this process (including interview notes and assessments) will be held as confidential. You will own the information generated, and I will maintain the strictest confidentiality. In addition, all interviews will be conducted in a confidential manner and the results will be presented in a blind format.

However, it is my expectation that you will share your insights and plans with appropriate people, including your boss. I can encourage and facilitate those meetings, if we decide that is appropriate. You will be responsible for initiating the meetings and determining what information you will share.

Next Steps
In order to proceed, I see several steps we must take:

- We will meet with your boss to discuss his interests.
- You and I should have another conversation after the meeting with your boss to finalize interviewee selections and interview protocol.
- After we finalize interviewee selections, I will wait for your approval to contact them for scheduling. This approval will signify that you have requested their participation and that they are expecting a call from my office.

I look forward to working with you on this project. Based on our initial conversations, I anticipate that our time together will be productive.

Sincerely,

[Your coach]

SAMPLE 4

Contract, Sponsor's Version

Date

[Kay Bradford's boss]

Dear [name],

The following is a letter of agreement regarding the coaching project for Kay Bradford. This letter describes goals, activities, roles, confidentiality, and terms. I will ask you to return a signed copy to indicate that you have reviewed and agree with the project parameters described here.

Goals
This coaching process is intended to help Kay enhance her leadership effectiveness in her current role and her viability as a candidate for broader roles. To this end, we will work toward the following general goals:

- Give Kay a clear understanding of her leadership behavior, style, and impact, focusing on core strengths, limitations, and development needs
- Identify challenges in her current and emerging roles, and explore possible gaps between her skills and those challenges
- Identify areas in which to focus Kay's development over the next year to increase her effectiveness
- Implement this plan by developing specific behaviors in critical situations and relationships

We identified specific development interests through initial contracting meetings with you and Kay. She would benefit from working on the following skills:

- Demonstrating a stronger leadership presence
- Thinking more strategically in real time with customers and colleagues
- Improving efficiency by focusing, prioritizing, and finding time for the most important activities

- Managing her team's performance and challenging team members to practice and demonstrate stronger analytical rigor
- Improving her relationship with her key client

The critical measure of success will be the key client's increased confidence in Kay, which will set the stage for her to take on increased responsibilities.

Activities
My approach to accomplishing the goals will include the following activities:

- Collecting interview-based, 360-degree feedback
- Administering selected assessment instruments
- Preparing and delivering a comprehensive leadership feedback report
- Analyzing feedback and creating a customized development plan
- Conducting ongoing coaching, which may include skill building, role negotiation, developing and debriefing leadership dialogues, and action plans
- Planning for (and conducting if appropriate) assessment of impact

Your Role
As we agreed, you play an essential role in supporting Kay's development. Specifically, I see three critical points in which your involvement will be valuable:

- Participating in an interview about your perceptions of Kay's leadership strengths and limitations
- Meeting with Kay and myself after she creates her development plan, to review key insights and action areas and to negotiate mutual expectations moving forward
- Meeting with Kay at the end of the process to review progress and future development plans

In addition, you agreed to provide Kay with direct feedback on an ongoing basis, as you observe her behaving either consistently or inconsistently with your expectations.

Confidentiality

All information generated during this process (including interview notes and assessments) is held as confidential. Kay will own the feedback report, and I will maintain the strictest confidentiality. In addition, all interviews will be conducted in a confidential manner and the results will be presented in a blind format.

However, it is my expectation that Kay will share her insights and plans with appropriate people, including you. I can encourage and facilitate those meetings, if we decide that is appropriate. Kay will be responsible for initiating the meetings and determining what information she will share.

Terms

The consulting fees for this project are X dollars and will be billed in mutually agreed-upon installments.

In addition, we charge reasonable and necessary travel expenses, as well as administrative expenses, including material preparation and communications. Invoices are submitted at the close of the month and are payable within thirty days of receipt.

I believe that this letter of agreement accurately reflects the project parameters we discussed. If you concur, please indicate your acceptance by your signature below and return a signed copy to me. If you have any questions or comments, now or at any time during this process, please do not hesitate to contact me. I look forward to working with you on this project.

_____   _____
Boss / Boss's organization   Coach / Coach's organization

cc: Human resources manager

SUMMARY

Key Activities of the Contracting Phase

Key Activity	Action Steps	Desired Outcomes
Sponsor-coach meeting	• Identify sponsor's goals for coaching • Describe coaching process • Agree on sponsor's role • Test sponsor's willingness to proceed	• Sponsor understands and agrees with process • Sponsor agrees on expected activities • Coach understands sponsor's goals for executive's development • Sponsor commits to proceed
Executive-coach meeting	• Identify executive's goals for coaching • Describe coaching process • Discuss expectations of executive • Test executive's willingness to proceed • Begin planning next steps	• Executive understands and agrees with process • Coach understands executive's development interests • Executive assesses coach's capability and style • Executive commits to proceed
Executive-sponsor-coach meeting	• Discuss sponsor's and executive's goals for coaching • Review process (if needed) • Share interests and concerns • Agree on desired outcomes and measures • Agree on roles and expectations	• All understand different goals • All agree on desired outcomes and measures • All agree on roles • All make final commitment to proceed • Executive has some new insights about sponsor's view of performance and capability

SUMMARY cont'd

Key Activity	Action Steps	Desired Outcomes
Coach assessment	• Determine executive's commitment to change behavior • Determine sponsor's commitment to reconsider judgments	• Coach commits to proceed
Delivery of contract	• Share contracts with executive and sponsor, and test agreements	• Contract and scope of work are formally approved

6

Insight

Assessment of Current Leadership Style

One of the most valuable elements of a coaching process is personalized feedback. Most executives don't get authentic feedback about how they're perceived or the effects of their behavior on others, and they don't reflect much on the underlying aspects of their character or personality that drive their behavior.

This chapter explains the objectives, key activities, and output of the second phase of a coaching engagement, gaining insight. In this step, your coach collects feedback to share with you, and then you jointly use it to create a customized development plan.

OBJECTIVES

The insight phase is intended to accomplish the following objectives:

- Help you gain a clear understanding of your behavior, its impact on others, and the unique pattern of strengths, limitations, and biases we call *style*
- Clarify your development goals
- Design a development plan for moving toward those goals

KEY ACTIVITIES

The coach leads the initial key activities in this phase: selecting colleagues to interview about your behavior, clarifying conditions of anonymity and confidentiality, conducting interviews, gathering supporting information, and organizing and preparing feedback. You are jointly responsible for the subsequent activities: reviewing and interpreting feedback, drawing conclusions about feedback messages and implications, and creating a development plan.

Selecting Colleagues to Interview About Your Behavior

Incorporating multiple perspectives. No single individual holds the ultimate truth about your behavior. Each interviewee provides a single perspective, which is influenced by his or her personal history and specific relationship with you. It is important to gather feedback from a range of individuals who have played a variety of roles and have different relationships and experiences with you. The coach may ask you to select individuals by category, choosing, for example, a number of bosses, peers, reports, and internal clients.

Occasionally I encounter a boss who believes that he or she already knows the executive's development issues and wants me to accept his or her definition without conducting additional interviews. A good coach should be able to help the boss understand that his or her perspective is only one of many and represents only the boss's interests. To accept this perspective as gospel, and to encourage you to do so, would simply compel you to obey your boss while doing nothing to help you incorporate broader perspectives. Even if your boss does have some valid conclusions about your development needs, others may be able to contribute important observations and identify broader implications. Finally, for you to take responsibility for your own development, it is essential that you make choices about your development needs based on information from multiple sources.

Focusing on important relationships. Interviews can be a starting point for change in your relationships because they signal that you are interested in your colleagues' input and are willing to change. They also open the door for further discussions with colleagues, enabling you to share feedback and agree on expectations. Therefore, it is in your best interest to choose interviewees with whom you have important relationships.

Clarifying Conditions of Anonymity and Confidentiality

Anonymity and confidentiality are two very different things, but they sometimes overlap in the commitments the coach makes and the expectations you and your colleagues hold.

Guaranteeing (within limits) anonymity for interviewees. A key element of the feedback process is gathering narrative comments from interviewees. Guaranteeing anonymity for these individuals is one way to increase their candor, and certain provisions can support this commitment. Individuals' names should never be associated with their comments in feedback reports. Often the coach will aggregate interviewees' comments by category (e.g., peers, clients, reports) so that you can focus on how your behavior may vary depending on the type of relationship. In such cases, the coach may require a minimum number of interviewees per category to protect their anonymity—especially for direct reports, who may be particularly fearful of providing feedback that might be traced to them.

One important goal for the coach in collecting this feedback is to capture specific stories, examples, and descriptions of behavior, rather than general conclusions about you, because such conclusions are not useful unless they are linked to actual behaviors. However, if specific stories are recorded, you may be able to identify the respondent. Thus it is important to inform interviewees that detailed notes will be captured during the interview and that comments may be reproduced verbatim in the feedback report. Interviewees should be given the option of making comments off the record, which will either be kept out of the report or presented in an agreed-on form.

In some cases, such as when the interviewee is your boss or significant other, you may need to know who said what. These individuals may be asked to agree to having their names presented along with their comments.

Committing to confidentiality for the executive. An effective coach will usually assure you that all data gathered for the feedback report will be shared only with you because it is important for you to feel that your work with the coach is private. However, because you are embedded in a web of relationships and expectations, it's also important to involve interviewees and other key colleagues in the development process. The coach can help you resolve this dilemma by guiding you around what information to share in a written or verbal summary report about your insights and plans. This expectation should be made explicit in the contracting phase.

Conducting Interviews

Covering many dimensions of leadership. The interview protocol should cover the key dimensions of leadership. The coach should ask some general questions about the executive's strengths and limitations. Beyond that, every coach will use different questions, but they should all seek to comprehensively cover many dimensions of leadership. For example, interview protocols may address the executive's relationships with different groups (peers, reports, bosses) and how the executive makes decisions, handles emotions, collaborates with others, balances work and personal life, and thinks strategically.

Probing for strengths and limitations. Each individual's style involves a combination of related strengths and limitations. It's not useful to focus only on limitations—for example, your struggle with strategy. It is more meaningful to know that you struggle with strategy but are great at building rapport with people. You should get insight about both strengths to build on and limitations to address.

Identifying specific behaviors and their impact. Because interviewees' perceptions of you are subjective and shaped by their biases, it's necessary to elicit information about your specific behavior—not just judgments about you. This enables you to see exactly what you're doing that leads others to draw the conclusions they do.

Interviewing significant others in your personal life. Your leadership behavior and style—for example, how you communicate, make decisions, and handle conflict—are manifested in all your relationships, not just those at work. Your significant other is likely to have a deeper experience of you in these areas than anyone at work does. In addition, nonwork relationships can provide an important window into your key interests and values. Finally, many executives find value in applying their desired behaviors at home as well as at work. Therefore, your coach may seek input from your significant other, family members, or close friends.

Interviewing you about yourself. It is necessary to collect formal interview data from you about your self-perceptions, using the same interview questions posed to the other interviewees. Your coach can then compare your answers to the perceptions of others and clearly define similarities and differences. The interview questions will also get you thinking in new ways about your leadership. The coach may also conduct additional interviews with you to learn more about you—for example, your educational background, career history, and personal goals.

Gathering Supporting Information

Using psychological instruments. Your coach is likely to administer some psychological instruments. This step is very important because it will help you understand the fundamental style patterns that shape your behavior. Style has implications for how you characteristically gather information, make decisions, behave with other people, and handle conflict. For example, we use the *Myers-Briggs Type Indicator®* (MBTI®) assessment to look at cognitive style, the FIRO-B® tool to understand interpersonal behavior, and the *Thomas-Kilmann Conflict Mode Instrument* to learn about approaches to conflict. These instruments can help you identify your preferences in a nonjudgmental way, emphasizing that everyone has a unique combination of strengths and limitations and that there is no right or wrong profile.

Collecting a written history and background information. A written background form can solicit objective information, such as employment and education history, as well as subjective information. For example, it might ask you to describe important events in your work history, changes in your behavior and beliefs over the course of your career, and typical conflicts and frustrations. Many people can share information in writing that they may not be able to share verbally. This may be because they feel more comfortable writing important information than sharing it face to face, or because they think differently when alone and writing than when talking with another person. Often the objective information can yield unique insights. For example, one executive's career history showed that he was a "job jumper," although he downplayed the frequency of his job changes in face-to-face conversation.

Organizing and Preparing Feedback

The coach can present feedback from interviews in one of two ways: either interpreted by the coach or verbatim.

Considering advantages and disadvantages of interpreted feedback. With this option, the coach analyzes the interview material prior to the feedback meeting and then presents a summary feedback report organized by the themes he or she has identified, probably illustrated by interviewee quotes. This approach has the dual advantages of protecting interviewees' anonymity and making the feedback meeting more efficient. However, it adds a layer of bias from the coach's interpretation that may not be directly evident in the report. Also, you are less likely to accept conclusions that you didn't help create. Finally, this option can dilute the power of the unfiltered interviewee comments and stories.

Considering advantages and disadvantages of verbatim feedback. With this option, the coach presents undigested feedback organized by question and category. In this scenario, you and the coach sit and interpret the feedback together. This approach can be time-consuming, but it allows you to determine the meaning of the feedback for yourself—which makes it more likely you will be motivated to take action. My group considers this second option preferable, and I have based my description of the review of feedback on this option.

Reviewing and Interpreting Feedback

As you and the coach sit down together to review the feedback, the coach will set a framework for the discussion, such as the following:

- What comments are you surprised by? What comments confirm what you believed to be true?

- What are you pleased about? Concerned about?

- Do you see any themes or patterns emerging?

- What issues or comments do you wish to further clarify?

The coach should provide some questions to help you think about the meaning of the feedback you are about to receive and some information about the structure of the feedback meeting.

Carefully making meaning out of the feedback.

- The most important thing you must understand is that feedback from interviews is not the universal truth. It includes subjective perceptions, along with observed actions. Even the observed actions are usually attached to subjective judgments. These perceptions vary by individual and by group, partly because you may behave differently with different people, and partly because people have different biases and expectations. Individuals form perceptions based in part on their identity and the nature of their relationship with you, so you can see the different aspects of yourself that are present in several kinds of relationships. Do you have conflict with peers but not with bosses or reports? Do you treat your bosses deferentially but your reports tyrannically? The goal is to look for patterns.

- Others' views and expectations should not be treated as mandates. The goal of coaching is not to make you conform but rather to give you information you can use in making choices about how you wish to behave and the impact you wish to have on others.

- There are no perfect leaders. All leaders possess strengths and weaknesses, and all leaders can find specific ways to improve their effectiveness.

Understanding the kinds of issues revealed by feedback.

- Some feedback will reveal new information about others' expectations of you. Perhaps you were unaware of these expectations because you recently moved into a new role, or maybe you have not created strong feedback loops or been concerned with others' expectations.

- Some feedback will seem invalid. You may feel that others have misinterpreted your intent in a particular situation. If so, the coach's job is to help you understand how you may unintentionally be affecting others. If you simply label these others as wrong and decide you must correct their error, you will be missing out on a valuable opportunity to learn about yourself. In some cases, if an interviewee has a perception of you that is not shared by others, it may have more to do with the interviewee's biases than with your behavior. However, this interviewee may have identified a real issue that remains mostly hidden except in certain situations, so it is worth considering the possibility that his or her perceptions have some broader validity. Your coach will help you work through these questions. You may leave the feedback session with several questions like this that need to be further discussed with your colleagues. In addition, your coach can help you become more transparent about your intentions when you interact with your colleagues, so that there is less room for misinterpretation in the future.

- Some feedback will highlight skills you need to develop. This often occurs in situations in which an executive has a new role with new demands, such as developing others or formulating strategy.

- Some feedback will reflect your enduring style: long-standing patterns of strengths and limitations that are based in your personal character, and typical ways that you handle certain situations or relationships that can be productive or unproductive. These patterns are unlikely to change fundamentally. However, with more insight, you can learn to make more effective choices. For example, you might steer away from certain roles that emphasize capabilities in which you are weak. Or you might choose to surround yourself with others who have complementary strengths, to compensate for your limitations.

- Some feedback will reflect your perspective. If so, what seems like a fundamental style issue can perhaps be transcended. For example, executives who fear challenging their clients' expressed needs may be averse to conflict. However, once they gain a broader view of their role and the value of challenging clients and helping clients see their needs differently, they may cease to see this challenge as a source of conflict; rather, they may realize that it can lead to even stronger relationships.

Using instrument feedback to illuminate style issues. Psychological instruments can help you understand some of the aspects of your basic style that shape how you behave, such as your preferences re-garding interaction, problem solving, communication, and conflict management.

Following key principles for the conversation during the feedback meeting. Most coaches believe the goal of this session is for you to absorb the feedback and to start to make sense of it—not to draw conclusions. The time for interpretation and action plans will come later. The primary focus of the discussion is to review the feedback together, share reactions, and discuss implications. The more you can verbalize your reactions and discuss them with your coach, the more you are likely to learn and the more helpful your coach can be to you.

Drawing Conclusions About Feedback Messages and Implications

At the end of the feedback session, the coach will probably ask you to reflect on the feedback and its meaning for some period of time, typically a couple of weeks or so. Your coach, who will reflect on these same matters, will probably give you some questions to con-sider during that time. You should think about what you have learned about yourself and what changes you wish to make. Your conclusions will serve as input into the development planning process. Sample 5 shows one example of an assignment that both coach and executive should complete in the weeks between the feedback meeting and the upcoming planning meeting.

Creating a Development Plan

After these weeks of reflection, you will again meet with the coach. Each of you will bring your prework to the table, to be used as the basis for creating a consensus development plan that will guide the rest of the coaching process. It will also be the framework for dis-cussing the process with others. The plan is not intended to be set in stone; instead, it is a working document that will be periodically

---

SAMPLE 5

Coach/Executive Prework for Planning Session

What are your major insights about your leadership?
- *Key strengths:* behaviors that you perform skillfully and that support your effectiveness
- *Development needs:* behaviors that you could improve that would enhance existing strengths
- *Key limitations:* behaviors that are "stuck" or stalled due to personal history

What are your interests for development?
- Vision/desired outcomes of development
- Behaviors you wish to change

What key situations can you use to implement new behaviors?
- Relationships
- Projects
- Strategies

---

revisited and revised as needed. A thorough plan should include the following elements.

Summarizing insights about your current leadership. At a minimum, this summary should include your major strengths and limitations and important aspects of your personal style.

Noting issues that require further testing. These issues might include areas of contradictory or ambiguous feedback.

Articulating your short-term vision. This exercise helps you envision yourself after a successful development process and should include your desired work context, how you wish to behave, the responses you wish to get from others, and the impact you will have.

Identifying specific behaviors you intend to change. These can include new skills or behaviors you wish to develop, old behaviors you wish to stop using, or behaviors you wish to continue using but more effectively.

Choosing key situations in which to implement the behaviors. This list may include important interactions, business initiatives or projects, or annual objectives. Any situation you face provides an opportunity to put new behaviors into practice.

Spelling out an agreement for the coaching relationship. You and your coach should lay out an explicit agreement for how the coaching time will be used and decide how much time will be spent on specific issues, such as raising and discussing emergent challenges, planning and debriefing interactions, and teaching and practicing key skills. The agreement may also define the frequency, duration, and format of coaching sessions. For example, my coaching group establishes biweekly meetings of sixty to ninety minutes and also asks the client to call between scheduled meetings to discuss important or time-sensitive issues, as well as emerging opportunities.

Reviewing your development plan with the sponsor. This is an important conversation because it helps you ensure that your plan is aligned with the sponsor's expectations for your development, and it also allows you to enlist the sponsor's support in your development. In addition, this conversation can have an impact on your relationship with your sponsor. Because this conversation falls at the boundary between the insight phase and the implementation phase, I'll discuss it more fully in the next chapter.

The key elements of a coaching plan include the following:

Vision (eight to twelve months in the future)

- Desired outcomes
- Desired new behaviors

Assessment of yourself in relation to vision

- Strengths that can help you

- Skills you need to develop

- Limitations that can hinder you

Implementation activities

- Key interactions, both planned and debriefed

- Principles for operating at each moment

- Skill-building activities such as training or coaching conversations

Role of coach

- Frequency and duration of meetings

- Agendas for meetings

Samples 6 and 7 show two development plans. The executives who produced these plans chose slightly different formats. Jamie Grady's development plan is an outline for his personal reference, while George Watts's development plan is in the form of a letter to key stakeholders, including his boss, and also provides the framework for his feedback meetings with each of them.

SAMPLE 6

Jamie Grady's Development Plan

Summary of Current Leadership Strengths and Limitations

Strengths
- Delivering on key projects
- Building relationships with clients
- Being responsive to clients' stated needs
- Tailoring communication to the audience
- Remaining calm in tense situations
- Being easygoing
- Facilitating consensus decisions
- Conceptualizing and analyzing issues
  Result: Working well with others and satisfying clients

SAMPLE 6 cont'd

Limitations
- Influencing primarily in one-on-one meetings, not in public forums
- Inability to directly confront conflicts
- Inability to challenge clients on their view of their needs
- Inability to build informal relationships with senior clients
- Not having a long-term vision for desired impact on the business
    Result: Missed opportunities to influence, have impact, and achieve objectives

Development Goals
- Confronting issues rather than avoiding them or handling them off-line
- Being more influential in relationships
- Reshaping project X

Opportunities to Practice Desired Behaviors
- Asking for needed support from my boss
- Managing my reports' performance
- Engaging senior clients, agreeing on a role for value creation

Strategies for Developing
- Planning to implement my development goals in relevant interactions
- Acting and observing
- Debriefing interactions
- Creating a daily mantra and identifing opportunities to manifest it
- Understanding and managing inertia and resistance
- Identifying and learning skills and models
- Knowing my personal vision and testing congruence with behavior

Measures of Success
- Feeling less overloaded
- Contributing more input
- Approaching clients with ideas
- Telling clients that changes are required on their part
- Implementing project X
- Influencing others

SAMPLE 6 cont'd

Long-Term Vision
- Solving problems
- Building consensus
- Associating with smart people
- Having fun
- Having time for family
- Having time for music

Elements of a Mantra
- Identifying interests in every situation
- Understanding problems with confrontation, thinking about consequences of confronting
- Reframing confrontations

OUTPUT

This phase results, tangibly, in the development plan I've described. Intangibly, it results in a shared picture that you, your coach, and the sponsor hold for the specific focus and outcome of the implementation phase.

Having this clear picture, both of yourself as you are now and of yourself as you wish to be, is an important step that can help you see the world differently and behave in different ways. However, insight by itself is far from enough to produce lasting behavior change. Now comes the critical challenge of implementing that lasting change.

SAMPLE 7

George Watts's Development Plan

Date
To: [Boss, Key Stakeholders]
From: George Watts
Regarding: Leadership Development

This year, I began a leadership development program with the help of a coach. My goal is to be as effective as I can be. We have completed the first phase in the program, which has involved

- Assessing my current leadership through interviews with you and others, and through instruments that define my leadership style

- Reviewing this material, identifying key patterns and themes in my current leadership, and establishing a focus for my development over the next several months

I have found this process to be very valuable. In this letter I will describe my insights and plans. I have scheduled a meeting with you to review these and to hear your thoughts and insights.

Leadership Strengths
The feedback revealed the following leadership strengths to build on:

- Clarifying vision and direction for my group
  - Thinking ahead, identifying direction and communicating it
  - Identifying key departmental priorities and success factors
  - Conceptualizing and thinking strategically
  - Thinking beyond own group to organization-wide issues and needs

- Understanding and tackling complex issues
  - Developing processes to address issues
  - Being a leader and resource

- Building my credibility and reputation
  - Remaining impartial
  - Speaking directly
  - Sharing valuable input

- Infusing energy and drive into my team
  - Raising enthusiasm and mobilizing people's energy
  - Consistently endorsing high standards and quality
  - Having a lot of energy and getting a lot done

SAMPLE 7 cont'd

The consequence of the above strengths is that I have built an organization that is strong in many respects.

Leadership Limitations
The following limitations were identified and need to be addressed:
- Not always collaborating
  - Not listening to input of individuals whom I don't respect
  - Not listening when I've made up my mind
  - Presenting my point of view aggressively, leaving no room for discussion
  - Not building support for my decisions
- Not developing people sufficiently
  - Not delegating and empowering enough
  - Micromanaging
  - Not valuing different styles and approaches
- Not directly addressing conflicts
  - Discussing people conflicts with others rather than with the individual directly
  - Going around people if I can't get agreement on an issue
- Setting standards too high and applying the same level of rigor to all things

The consequences of these limitations are that people don't buy into my decisions and that people don't develop to their fullest potential around me, which causes me to exert tighter control. I believe that the core issue is treating others with respect and honoring their perspective. This is a value I hold, although I realize that it conflicts with my strong desire to get things done and to get them done right, and that often I have chosen getting things done as a higher priority.

Proposed Development Plan
This development plan is focused on helping me develop skills to improve my leadership effectiveness, specifically valuing others more and building consensus.
- Holding meetings with interviewees
  - Sharing key insights and plans, and discussing future expectations
  - Asking for ongoing feedback
- Receiving training on key skills from my coach
  - Working on collaborating, managing expectations, and influencing

SAMPLE 7 cont'd

- Planning work interactions, practicing skills in real settings, and debriefing key interactions with coach
- Focusing on strategically important situations and challenges where consensus is needed
- Seeing setbacks as an opportunity to understand the forces that are driving my behavior

I also plan to make my leadership development as transparent as possible, in hopes that I can be a model for self-awareness and self-development in my group. I believe that this will help create a learning organization and will help me address my own development issues.

I look forward to discussing these issues with you. I also plan to review this plan with my human resources manager and incorporate her input.

SUMMARY

Key Activities of the Insight Phase

Key Activity	Action Steps	Desired Outcomes
Interviewee selection	Executive: • Chooses range of respondents • Focuses on important relationships	Executive: • Gains multiple perspectives on behavior and impact • Has starting point for changing important relationships
Clarification of anonymity and confidentiality	Coach: • Guarantees anonymity of interviewees • Commits to confidentiality of executive	• Executive receives candid feedback from all interviewees
Leadership interviews	Coach: • Covers many dimensions of leadership • Probes for both strengths and limitations • Probes for specific behaviors and impact • Interviews (if possible) significant others in executive's personal life • Interviews executive about himself or herself	Executive: • Gets comprehensive picture of leadership behavior • Understands how views vary across groups • Can recognize gaps between self-perceptions and others' perceptions
Gathering of supporting information	Coach asks executive to: • Fill out psychological instruments • Provide written history and background information	• Executive gains insight into deeper character issues than interviews alone can provide

SUMMARY cont'd

Key Activity	Action Steps	Desired Outcomes
Feedback organization and preparation	Coach considers: • Advantages and disadvantages of interpreted feedback • Advantages and disadvantages of verbatim feedback	• Executive accepts feedback insights and commits to consequent action
Feedback meeting	• Coach establishes key principles for the feedback meeting conversation • Coach prepares executive to carefully make meaning out of the feedback • Coach prepares executive to understand the kinds of issues revealed by feedback • Coach and executive review interview feedback • Coach and executive use instrument feedback to illuminate style issues	• Executive gains deeper understanding of leadership strengths and limitations
Reflection on conclusions	Executive and coach individually: • Reflect on feedback messages and implications • Respond to several structured questions	• Executive reaches clarity on current style and development goals

Key Activity	Action Steps	Desired Outcomes
Creation of development plan	Coach and executive jointly: • Summarize insights about executive's current leadership • Note issues that require further testing • Articulate short-term vision • Identify specific behaviors executive will change • Choose key situations in which to implement new behaviors • Spell out agreement for the coaching relationship • Review development plan with sponsor	Executive, sponsor, and coach: • Have joint agreement about development goals, methods, roles, and measures • Share a commitment to implementing development plan

7

Implementation

Development of New Perspective and Skills

This chapter explains the objectives, key activities, and output of the third phase of a coaching engagement, in which the coach helps you implement the development plan.

Ideally, your coach will have begun coaching conversations based on your initial goals immediately after the contracting phase. However, once the feedback and planning sessions are completed, these conversations take on a clearer direction that is shaped by the development plan.

OBJECTIVES

The implementation phase is intended to accomplish the following objectives:

- Get you to practice and adapt new behaviors in a structured way to internalize them
- Reach development goals
- Reshape stakeholders' perceptions

KEY ACTIVITIES

The key activities of this phase follow a sequence intended to implement and tailor new behaviors in a way that fits your individual style. They are also intended to get maximum impact out of behavior change by ensuring that others see the change and that the new behaviors are employed in important work situations and in professional relationships.

Preparing Others for Change

An important element is to prepare others to recognize and accept the changes that you expect to make. The first step is to meet with colleagues to share your insights from their feedback and your development goals, and to negotiate any new expectations for relationships. This meeting can be valuable for several reasons. It signals to colleagues that you take their feedback seriously and want to do something about it, and confirms that your development plan is in fact addressing issues that colleagues see as important. It also gives you the chance to practice behaviors that are typically new to executives, such as openly sharing information about yourself and asking others about their expectations. The meeting allows you to test your perceptions of how effectively you are changing. It also creates some pressure for you to follow through on promised changes, because you've made your commitment explicit to others. Finally, it gives you the opportunity to enlist others' support for your change effort.

Typically, this conversation has four basic elements:

- Sharing your insights from the feedback and testing them
- Reviewing your development plan and testing it to ensure commitment
- Discussing any new expectations
- Negotiating for feedback and other support during your change effort

It is especially important to have this conversation with your direct manager. In fact, my group doesn't consider a development plan complete until the executive has met with his or her boss to review it. Sample 8 shows a typical script for the feedback meeting with an executive's manager.

SAMPLE 8

Executive's Script for Manager Feedback Meeting

Objectives
- Give your manager an understanding of your insights about your leadership and plans for development
- Ensure that your plans are consistent with your manager's expectations
- Signal to your manager your interest in learning, growing, and being more effective

Agenda
- Thank manager for providing input
- Review key insights from the feedback
  - Check against manager's perceptions
- Review goals and plans for behavior change
  - Include actions taken to date
  - Check against manager's interests
- Agree on desired outcomes and measures
- Discuss support needed from manager (e.g., ongoing feedback)

Roles
- Coach (if attending meeting)
  - Does not share content of your feedback
  - Defines the framework for discussion
  - Facilitates as needed
- You
  - Schedule meeting
  - Decide what to share (and not share)
  - Review insights, goals, and plans
  - Ask for manager's views
  - Suggest measures
  - Ask for desired support
- Manager
  - Reacts to insights and plans
  - Agrees on measures and ongoing support

It is also valuable to have a similar conversation with other important colleagues; Sample 9 shows a typical script for this conversation. It is not terribly different from the type of conversation you would have with your direct manager, except that your manager has a more formal role in reviewing your development plan and supporting the implementation of your goals.

Some executives avoid initiating these conversations with colleagues because they think that their development is private or that discussing it makes them appear weak. However, your colleagues are likely to know that you are going through this process—especially if they were interviewed—and they might already hold some expectations to see you change. If you don't talk about it with them, they may assume that you are doing nothing.

SAMPLE 9

Executive's Script for Colleague Engagement Meetings

Objectives
- Give the colleague an understanding of your insights about your leadership and plans for development
- Ensure that your insights and plans are consistent with the colleague's perceptions and expectations
- Signal to the colleague your interest in learning, growing, and being more effective

Agenda
- Thank colleague for providing input if he or she was one of the interviewees
- Share key insights about your leadership
  - Check against colleague's perceptions
- Review goals and plans for behavior change
  - Include actions taken to date
  - Check against colleague's interests
- Ask for any specific expectations the colleague has of you
- Share any expectations you have of the colleague
  - Discuss support for your development, such as ongoing feedback
  - Discuss colleague's behaviors that will help you be more effective
- Agree on mutual actions

If you feel uncomfortable with a formal feedback meeting, talk with your coach. There may be another way to signal your changes to co-workers and to get them involved. For example, Peter McCall found it easier to introduce the issue at the end of a work meeting with a colleague. He told the colleague that he had tried some new behaviors in the meeting and asked the colleague for specific feedback on those behaviors. In other words, how you engage your colleagues in your development can be tailored to fit your style and still address the goals of demonstrating desire to change, receiving feedback on others' perceptions of your efforts, and helping others begin seeing you differently.

Identifying Development Opportunities

A development opportunity is any situation in which you can pursue your purpose and practice new skills. Virtually every major work situation—an important project, new relationship, or new strategy to be implemented—offers several development opportunities. Furthermore, almost any situation, no matter how minor it appears, may be a development opportunity, if you have the ability to recognize it.

Your coach should help you learn to notice these opportunities by developing a capability that we call *situational awareness.* We define this as the ability to describe the type of situation you are observing so you have the chance to utilize it. Unless you can recognize the type of situation, it can be difficult to determine how to best advance your purpose and practice new skills. Are you trying to resolve a conflict? Do you wish to influence someone? Or are you trying to build consensus for a plan of action? An effective coach will help you learn to ask and answer questions such as, "What is happening in this situation?" and "What do others want out of this situation?"

For example, Suzanne Jacobs identified her relationship with her senior client as a major development opportunity. Specifically, she wished to build a different kind of relationship with him, in which he felt that Suzanne deeply understood his goals and challenges and could help him meet them. Every interaction with this client—whether face-to-face, by phone, or in writing—became an opportunity to reshape that relationship.

Clarifying Purpose and Interests

Once you recognize a development opportunity, the next step is to decide how to use that opportunity. You are more likely to use the opportunity effectively if you are clear about what you want to accomplish. There are two important sources of information you can draw on to make an effective choice: your general purpose at work and your personal development plan.

In the typical mastery-oriented executive world, it can be difficult for you to clarify and stay in touch with your own purpose and interests, such as what you want to contribute, how you want to behave, and how you don't want to behave. Before you can apply your purpose in every situation, you need to understand it in a very broad way. To help executives clarify this broad purpose, we have them develop a personal purpose statement of desired behaviors, attitudes, and effects, which they should keep in mind every day. This statement should be concise and can include answers to questions such as the following:

- How do I want to act?

- What new behaviors do I want to practice?

- What impact do I want to have on the organization and on others around me?

- Where should I focus my time and attention?

Samples 10 and 11 are personal purpose statements from Ed Romaine and Tom Alessandro.

Once your personal purpose is clear, your coach can teach you how to think about your purpose and development goals in every situation, using questions such as the following:

- How can I act in this situation that will be consistent with my purpose?

- What opportunities exist in this situation to practice new behaviors?

- How can I frame the situation so others can understand my purpose?

- How can I get others to support my purpose?

SAMPLE 10

Ed Romaine's Personal Purpose Statement

A Plan for How I Want to Operate at Every Moment

- Know my interests and share them with relevant others
  - Determine my specific interests in terms of outcomes and process of getting there
  - Determine my general purpose and how I can use the situation to move toward it

- Establish a shared framework for moving forward in new or ambiguous situations
  - Decide where we are trying to go
  - Know what we need to learn
  - Agree on how to discuss our interests when we know them

- Become aware of and surface conflicts and concerns

- Ask myself questions when I find myself being quiet or passive
  - Understand my current interests
  - Understand my current concerns

Planning Behavior in Specific Situations

Now that you have identified an opportunity and clarified your interests, you can decide what you will say and do specifically in this situation to take advantage of the opportunity.

SAMPLE 11

Tom Alessandro's Personal Purpose Statement

Guiding Principles to Become the Person I Want to Be

- Relax
- Focus on the important things
- Empower and develop others
- Give others responsibility

Daily Tactics
- Ensure communication is two-way in meetings
  - Don't assume I always know the answer or have all the information
  - Ask for input, reactions, ideas
  - LISTEN
- Support reports who act in a self-directed way
  - Take the opportunity to say, for example, "I didn't need you to ask my approval about that" when they come to me for my input or approval
  - Share all my expectations in the beginning for a completed task
- Use others' strengths to support me
  - Get X's help in producing written memos
  - Use meeting facilitator
- Monitor my stress and stop myself before getting to the volatile point
  - Take a break and ask myself what is going on, or exercise
- Never say yes immediately to requests to take on a task
  - Critically look at whether I can do it

Preparations
- Visualize my day in advance
- Remind myself how I want to operate
- Review my principles before I enter a meeting
- Bring these notes and refer to them often

Creating scripts for action. The coach can help you concretely plan how you will act in these situations to satisfy your interests. A script aids in developing and internalizing new habits and generally includes the following:

- Framing, or defining the purpose for, the interaction

- Sharing your own interests in or objectives for the interaction

- Soliciting others' interests in the interaction

- Discussing proposed actions that integrate interests and testing commitment

Rehearsing your script. This step helps you try out a script with a skilled and supportive listener. Rehearsing helps you to learn what part of the new behavior feels comfortable and what part will be difficult or will make you nervous.

Anticipating obstacles. A skilled coach can use insight from feedback to help you anticipate and prepare for difficulties in implementing the desired behaviors that may result from your personal style, ingrained interaction patterns, or others' reactions to you.

Using your coach for just-in-time planning. Whenever you identify a development opportunity, you can benefit by contacting your coach and talking about the situation and how to approach it. Some executives are reluctant to call their coach too often outside scheduled meeting times, but most coaches will welcome the opportunity to talk with you in real time, when you're facing actual dilemmas. Doing so gives them more opportunities to help you apply new behaviors and perspectives to concrete situations where it can have an impact.

Acting and Observing the Effect

At this point, you must take the action you mapped out earlier and say or do something. It is important to observe your own actions carefully and concretely, as well as thoughts and feelings you have at the time, as these become important indicators about inner forces that support or impede the behaviors you wish to exhibit.

An important element of coaching that is necessary to help sustain change is to teach you to evaluate your performance and impact on an ongoing basis and to use this awareness to adapt your behavior. You can start developing this capability by reflecting on your actions and their alignment with your purpose and interests.

Debriefing Actions and Outcomes

This debriefing occurs between you and your coach, as part of the coaching conversation. In this conversation you should be sure to do the following:

- Refocus on your development goals and interests
- Describe the situations you have encountered, both planned and unplanned, and your actions in those situations
  - The meaning or significance of the situation
  - Your purpose or interests in the situation
  - A description of your action and its impact on others
    - Areas of alignment with development interests
    - Areas of conflict (e.g., backsliding, old behaviors)
- Identify dilemmas and places where you are stuck
- Reframe the situation and consider other perspectives
- Plan and rehearse subsequent actions
  - Strengthen the forces that caused positive outcomes
  - Recognize and manage forces that blocked your desired action

Sample 12 shows one script for a coaching conversation.

Continually Engaging Stakeholders

Several purposes are served by engaging others in your development.

SAMPLE 12

Coach's/Executive's Script for a Coaching Conversation

Before Meeting
- Coach reviews goals and action plans
- You execute agreed-on action steps and anticipate future opportunities

At Meeting
- Coach and you revisit coaching focus (as needed)
- You describe situations faced, actions taken, and any other relevant factors
  - Your purpose and interests
  - What worked well (aligned with vision)
  - What didn't work well (conflicting with vision)
  - Dilemmas or opportunities
  - Your interests now
- Coach examines the conflicts
  - Their meaning to you
  - What you have tried
  - What you are trying to accomplish
  - What's frustrating
  - What's your contribution to the problem
- Coach helps you reframe the situation and opportunities for action
  - New perspectives
  - Potential new action steps
- You rehearse new behavior

After Meeting
- You take agreed-on action
- You observe and record effects

Understanding their interests in your behavior and actions. Simply asking others what they expect from you can be a powerful intervention in your relationship with them. Understanding and managing others' expectations does not mean you are mandated to conform to them in all respects, but it does enable you to reach explicit agreements on how you can handle these expectations.

Testing your perceptions of your behavior and its impact. Your views of how your behavior is changing aren't necessarily reliable. You can get useful information by asking others to share feedback with you on specific behaviors when they have opportunities to observe you.

Helping others see you differently. As important as it is for you to change your behavior, it is also important to change how others see you. Others can be locked into old views about your behaviors and the motives behind those behaviors. You can help them see you differently by discussing what you are trying to do and why, and by sharing the progress you are making.

Helping others treat you differently. Virtually all executives, not just those who are seen as having performance issues, are trying to modify something about how they are perceived in the organization. For example, Jamie Grady's clients perceived him as great at execution, delivering the systems they requested. However, he wished to shift his relationship with them so that they would stop dictating solutions and instead treat him as a strategic partner who could help them identify solutions. Treating him in this way would mean inviting him to meetings he hadn't attended before, sharing more information with him, entertaining his proposals, and enabling him to have an entirely different kind of impact. One thing he did to achieve this end was simply talk to his clients about the different way he wanted to work with them and why.

Helping others see "hiccups" in development as inevitable. No development process moves in a straight line of progress. All clients, even the ones who develop the most successfully, experience missteps, side steps, or even backsliding, which can lead others to conclude that the desired changes are not occurring, especially if the original reason for the coaching was a performance problem. However, it is possible to anticipate challenges and encourage others to share their concerns when hiccups occur, so you can address them.

SAMPLE 13

Executive's Script for a Progress Review with Sponsor

Objectives
- Make visible to your sponsor the changes you are making
- Ensure that these changes are consistent with your sponsor's expectations
- Receive any input or observations your sponsor may have about changes in you

Agenda
- Review original goals
- Summarize development to date: activities, behaviors, outcomes
- Discuss continuing development needs and progress yet to be made
- Discuss and agree on next steps, measures, support, and any modification of development plan

---

Reviewing your progress. Engaging others in your development provides you with an opportunity to address a common challenge that all executives face: namely, ensuring that clients see your work as valuable to *them.*

It is especially important to engage your boss or sponsor in this way. To accomplish this, you may choose to hold formal quarterly meetings to review your development progress, with the coach's presence optional. Sample 13 is a typical script for such a progress meeting with the sponsor.

Managing Your Resistance

You should expect resistance not only from others but from yourself as well.

Anticipating patterns that may hinder desired behaviors. Like any executive trying to implement new behaviors, you are likely to have some old patterns that get in the way. You behave as you do for a reason—either you get some benefit from it or you think you will, and your assumptions about the effects of acting differently are likely to hinder change. These assumptions usually are visible in how you talk to yourself and others about the implications of your behavior or the risks of changing. The coach must work with you to decode this self-talk and to replace it with new beliefs that reinforce the desired behaviors. For example, do you believe that others will reward you for the old behavior, or punish you for the new behavior?

Recognizing and understanding backsliding. Slipping back into old behaviors is inevitable, especially when you are tired, under pressure, or interacting in relationships where there is a long history of issues. It's important to look at these situations not as failures but as learning opportunities, and to expect that you will need to make repeated attempts to integrate new behavior. You should try to identify what happened just before the backslide occurred. Often, red flags come in the form of emotional reactions, such as anger or anxiety. Your coach can help you recognize these emotions, step back, and understand them—rather than simply reacting to them. For example, one executive who had made many changes in his behavior still found himself reactively arguing with others when he felt they were challenging him. Once he recognized this trap, he was able to perceive when he began to feel defensive and consciously make the decision to inquire about others' perspectives instead of arguing with them.

Cleaning up mistakes when they happen. If backsliding is unavoidable, then what matters most is how you handle it afterward. You can go back to people to apologize and replay the conversation. You can also publicly commit to strategies to avoid backsliding in the future and ask for your colleagues' help. If the mistake occurred during a project, you can offer to redo the work in a different way. What is important is being transparent about the mistake and your intention to correct it.

Helping colleagues put mistakes into context. Often, especially if there is an identified performance problem, stakeholders may be tempted to seize on any episode of backsliding as evidence that the executive is not changing sufficiently. It's important that both you and your coach have explicit conversations with stakeholders about this temptation and reset their expectations to take into account that mistakes are going to be made, even in the best of circumstances.

Kay Bradford was trying to improve her client's satisfaction with how she was addressing his needs at a strategic level. Several months into this effort, her team made a presentation to this client that was not up to his desired standard. His first reaction was to conclude, and to report to her boss, that she had not improved at all, although in the intervening months she had indeed provided more rigorous and strategic contributions. She decided to talk to her client and own up to her mistakes by discussing the reasons why she had not paid sufficient attention to this presentation. She then committed to redoing the plan in a way that satisfied his expectations. She also asked for his help in the future, arranging for him to sit down with her to discuss his expectations and her thoughts to ensure alignment before she developed any major proposal.

Being wary of "flight into health." This is a frequent form of resistance, and it works like this: You have been working with your coach for a few months and you think you're doing better on your development areas. You start canceling meetings with your coach, and stop calling to get help preparing for situations, because you think you no longer need the help. This is a natural reaction to an emotional process occurring inside you, which protects you from facing difficult or painful issues. Your way of operating took years to evolve, and you've developed lots of internal mechanisms to protect it. Like everyone, you want to feel in control of yourself, and you don't want to get hurt or fail or lose others' esteem. It's those wishes and fears that will likely drive your avoidance of the coaching process. Now, it is indeed possible that you are doing better, but you won't be wasting your coach's time if you continue to meet even though you feel you are successfully changing, and you could get some valuable insights.

The development cycle will be repeated many times over the course of your coaching engagement. As you practice new behaviors over and over, and experience the thoughts and feelings associated with them, you will start making a deeper shift in how you see yourself, other people, and your world. And your coach will gradually shift responsibility to you for managing the development cycle, in preparation for the end of the coaching engagement.

OUTPUT

There are two primary outputs of this phase. The first is behavior change consistent with your intended areas of development, as well as with your core purpose and interests. The second is change in others' perceptions of you, specifically to see you as open to development and demonstrating new and valued leadership behaviors.

SUMMARY

Key Activities of the Implementation Phase

Key Activity	Action Steps	Desired Outcomes
Prepare others for change	Executive: • Meets with colleagues to share insights and plans • Negotiates for development support • Establishes new expectations for working together	• Executive confirms that plan will address important needs • Colleagues begin to see executive differently • Executive commits publicly to change • Colleagues commit to support executive's development
Identify development opportunities	Executive and coach jointly: • Analyze situations encountered • Decide how situations can be used as opportunities to practice new behaviors	• Executive understands clearly what kind of opportunity is present in any situation
Clarify purpose and interests	Executive gets help from coach to: • Clarify general purpose at work • Clarify desired behavior principles • Understand own interests in any given situation	• Executive is better able to choose action that is aligned with purpose and interests
Plan behavior in specific situations	Executive works with coach to: • Create scripts • Rehearse scripts • Anticipate obstacles	Executive is more likely to: • Be successful in implementing new behaviors • Satisfy own interests

SUMMARY cont'd

Key Activity	Action Steps	Desired Outcomes
Act and observe the effect	Executive: • Carries out the plan • Notices what works well, what is difficult, and how others react	• Executive enhances understanding of own behavior patterns and potential impediments to change
Debrief actions and outcomes	Executive and coach: • Discuss what happened • Identify dilemmas • Consider alternate perspectives • Adapt future actions	• Executive is likely to take increasingly effective action in future situations
Engage stakeholders	Executive talks with stakeholders to: • Understand stake-holders' interests in executive's actions • Test stakeholders' perceptions of change in executive • Help stakeholders see and treat executive differently • Help stakeholders anticipate hiccups in development • Review executive's progress	Executive: • Is better able to manage others' expectations • Understands others' perceptions and judgments • Has the opportunity to confront and change others' perceptions
Manage your resistance	Executive: • Anticipates patterns that may hinder change • Looks for backsliding • Cleans up mistakes • Speaks with colleagues to help them under-stand mistakes • Remains wary of "flight into health"	• Executive is able to change deeply rooted personal patterns that can limit development • Executive develops the ability to pro-actively use mistakes to support continued learning • Colleagues are more accepting of execu-tive's mistakes

8

Closure

Transition to Self-Development

In the final phase of a coaching engagement, the formal coaching relationship is concluded and you prepare to continue your self-development independent of your coach. This chapter describes the objectives, key activities and underlying assumptions, and output of this phase.

OBJECTIVES

The closure phase both ends your coaching process and begins the next stage of your development. Thus, its objectives relate both to getting closure on the process and to equipping you for the next stage.

Determining the Impact of the Coaching Process

Sponsors will typically be interested in assessing your progress and the coaching process, both to make decisions about you and to consider possible future use of the coaching process.

Building Your Capacity for Self-Development

Over the course of the coaching engagement, an effective coach will never do anything to encourage you to feel dependent. Rather, the coach should always be working to transfer development tools and skills to you so that, by the scheduled date of closure, you feel able to continue development in a self-managed way.

Involving the Sponsor in Your Development

The sponsor will play a critical role in supporting future change, so he or she should participate in concluding the coaching relationship and planning your continued development. This helps make the sponsor an ongoing ally in your effectiveness and success.

KEY ACTIVITIES

The key activities of this phase include assessing the impact of the coaching project, creating a self-development plan, learning self-development skills, and sharing your plan with stakeholders.

Assessing the Impact of the Coaching Project on Your Development

This process gives you a clear picture of your development progress to date and helps you identify what to focus on next. There are a few steps to keep in mind here.

Agreeing on how to measure impact. Impact can be evaluated through several measures. It is as important to agree on these measures as it is to conduct the evaluation, to help ensure shared expectations about what type and degree of change is possible. Following are some possible measures for a coaching project.

- Observable change in the behaviors that were identified as development needs

- Improvements on annual goals or other performance measures

- Ability to recover quickly from inevitable mistakes or backslides

- Awareness of and ability to manage your style

Deciding who will do the assessment. The coach can interview colleagues and share their feedback with you much in the same way that the original assessment was conducted, but with fewer questions. Alternatively, you can conduct some or all of these assessment interviews yourself, which would further help you build the skills of getting feedback from others.

Constructing the assessment. You can use simple questions, such as the following ones, to interview colleagues. These questions should address behavior change in your development areas, as well as other dimensions you have selected, and you should ask interviewees for specific examples, not just general judgments.

- What positive changes have you seen me make over the past year?

- What changes would you have liked to see, but didn't?

- Can you think of any situations where I demonstrated [name the selected behavior]? Were there situations where [name the behavior] was still an issue?

- Can you recall a situation where I slipped into an old behavior? How do you think I handled the situation?

- Have you observed me taking action to handle my limitations, for example, asking for help in those areas?

Improvement in organizational performance measures can be assessed by comparing objective results to those from previous years, although this can be tricky since performance is affected by so many factors.

Sharing results with stakeholders. Stakeholders can use results to make choices about your future role and opportunities, and also about using coaching for other executives.

Creating a Self-Development Plan

The act of creating this plan will help you become very clear about your personal goals. The plan should be simple enough that you can keep it in mind during the course of your working day, and it can take any form you wish, as it is primarily for your own benefit. To create this plan, you will probably need to do the following work.

Summarizing your understanding of your current state as a leader. You should identify your current strengths and limitations, as well as your development to date.

Articulating your vision for your leadership. Decide how you would like to behave, the impact you wish to have, the role you feel you should play, and the response you want to elicit from others.

Choosing a few key development areas for the next year. Choose areas that will move you toward your vision. Also consider the feedback you received during the coaching process and identify areas that complement or expand on the work you did during this process. For each area, it is helpful to describe specific behaviors you wish to implement in certain situations.

Planning how you will address internal resistance and seek support. You will want to identify internal tendencies that might conflict with your development goals so that you can prepare red flags and overcome these tendencies when they arise. You should also design a strategy for receiving ongoing feedback, training, and any other external support.

Checklist 3 lists key elements that a self-development plan should include, and Sample 14 shows an actual plan.

Elements of a
Self-Development Plan

☐ Key elements of your current leadership: strengths, limitations, and style
☐ Your leadership vision for yourself, including goals and purpose
☐ Your development to date
☐ Areas for future development
☐ Strategies for addressing these areas
  • Key situations
  • Key behaviors to practice
  • Potential obstacles to change and how they will be addressed
    – Inner obstacles
    – Outer obstacles
☐ Support needed from others
☐ Plan for obtaining ongoing feedback

Learning Self-Development Skills

Self-development skills will be critical to your continued growth and increasing effectiveness.

Understanding the cycle of development. The cycle involves knowing yourself and your purpose, identifying opportunities for action, planning action, taking action, reflecting on the action taken, and adapting future actions. This cycle is parallel to the one that the coach has been leading you through.

Practicing the cycle. You can begin taking responsibility for moving through this process while you are still working with your coach. As you practice this process, it will become more efficient and automatic. Figure 1 depicts the self-development cycle.

Sharing Your Plan with Stakeholders

Involving others is important for many reasons. It helps you test your own conclusions about your development progress to date and understand your future development needs. It also helps others continue to see you differently and remain committed to your success.

SAMPLE 14

Suzanne Jacobs's Self-Development Plan

Initial Insights About My Leadership
- Strengths
  - Paying attention to detail
  - Sharing project ownership and asking for help if needed
  - Committing and working hard
  - Acting in a nonthreatening manner
  - Listening well
  - Asking questions to understand issues deeply
  - Being dependable

- Limitations
  - Going off on tangents instead of focusing on big-picture issues
    - Diving into too many details
  - Coming across as unprepared or harried at times
  - Not explicitly managing expectations of team members or confronting them when they have missed expectations
  - Not building strong client relationships, especially with senior clients
    - Executing clients' ideas instead of influencing

Development Focus in the Past Year
- Establishing the habit of planning for meetings
  - Framing purpose, communicating information, and wrapping up
- Building solid relationships with key clients
  - Being a partner in strategic conversations
- Focusing on leading and coaching reports
- Communicating clearly and succinctly with a clear framework

Assessment of Progress and Development to Date
- Am seeing significantly improved client relationships
  - Involved in strategic meetings with X, who calls me seeking input
- Have clarified my role relative to reports on their projects
  - Am setting clear performance expectations and coaching them

Areas for Future Development
- Continuing to improve my planning
- Focusing on clarifying my communication
  - Setting a framework at opening and closing of meetings
  - Not diving into details
- Building strong relationship at strategic level with new client Y
- Taking responsibility for new project and focusing on facilitating and framing instead of diving into task

FIGURE 1

The Self-Development Cycle

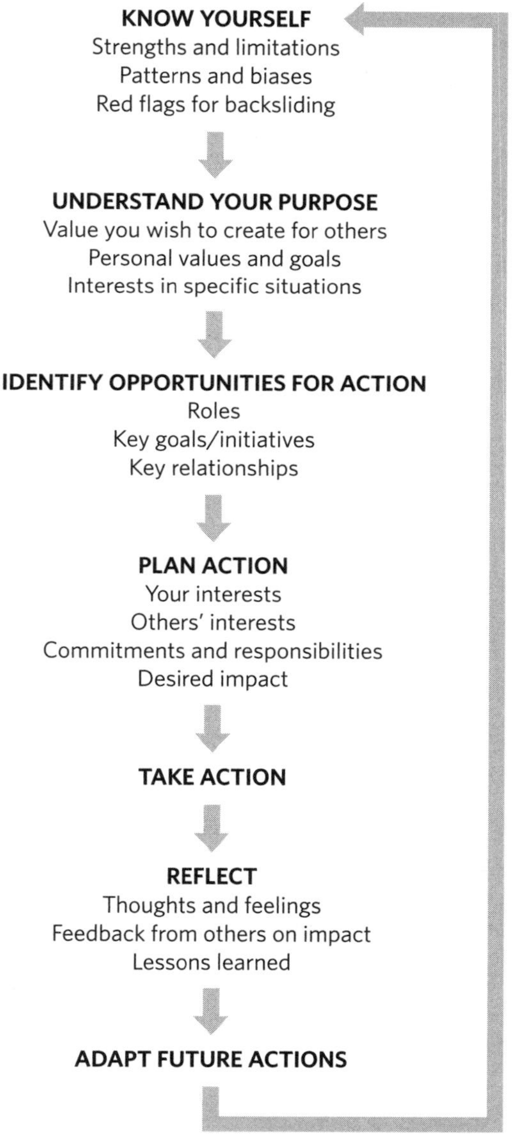

KNOW YOURSELF
Strengths and limitations
Patterns and biases
Red flags for backsliding

UNDERSTAND YOUR PURPOSE
Value you wish to create for others
Personal values and goals
Interests in specific situations

IDENTIFY OPPORTUNITIES FOR ACTION
Roles
Key goals/initiatives
Key relationships

PLAN ACTION
Your interests
Others' interests
Commitments and responsibilities
Desired impact

TAKE ACTION

REFLECT
Thoughts and feelings
Feedback from others on impact
Lessons learned

ADAPT FUTURE ACTIONS

You can involve various others, at different times, in the following ways.

Holding a closure meeting with your sponsor. In this meeting you can examine the results of your assessment to determine the impact of coaching. You can also review your self-development plan and seek your sponsor's input. To the extent that your plan involves support from your sponsor, this is the time to negotiate. Sample 15 shows a typical agenda for this meeting.

Sharing and testing your self-development plan with other key colleagues. Anyone who provided input during the coaching assessment and others who are important in your work might benefit from understanding your plan. As in the conversation with your sponsor, you can test your plan to make sure that it is consistent

---

SAMPLE 15

Executive's Agenda for a Closure Meeting with Sponsor

- Review original goals

- Summarize development progress: behavior change, skill development, and impact
  - Check sponsor's perceptions of your development

- Share self-directed development plan: goals, strategies, and measures
  - Check sponsor's reactions
  - Determine if plan addresses sponsor's interests
  - Incorporate any input from sponsor

- Agree on next steps, measures, and support
  - Discuss support needed from sponsor
  - Plan for future meetings
  - Decide how success will be measured

with your colleagues' interests and negotiate any specific expectations for how to work together in the future.

Checking progress periodically with your sponsor and other colleagues. You can do this at any time with any important colleague, in as abbreviated a fashion as you wish. The overall purpose is to check in with co-workers about their perceptions of your leadership, to hear any issues they may have, and to modify your development efforts based on what you learn.

OUTPUT

The primary tangible output of this phase is the self-development plan. The intangible output is your readiness to continue development in a self-directed manner. Although you are formally finished with the coaching process, your development is a lifelong journey. My hope is that coaching has provided you with the tools to continue revisiting and revising your vision and purpose, identifying areas in which you wish to develop, and bringing in additional resources and support as needed.

SUMMARY

Key Activities of the Closure Phase

Key Activity	Action Steps	Desired Outcomes
Assess impact of coaching engagement on executive's effectiveness	Executive and coach: • Agree on relevant measures of change • Decide who will do the assessment • Construct the assessment • Share results with stakeholders	Executive and stakeholders: • Have shared understanding about value of coaching process • Have shared understanding about executive's improvement on development goals
Create a self-development plan	Executive, with help of coach: • Summarizes understanding of current state as a leader • Articulates vision for own leadership • Chooses a few key development areas for the next year • Plans how to address resistance and seek support	Executive: • Has a simple plan to guide self-directed development • Is more likely to continue development progress into the future
Learn self-development skills	Coach ensures that executive: • Understands the cycle of development • Practices the cycle	• Executive increases capability to direct own development on an ongoing basis
Share self-development plan with stakeholders	Executive: • Holds closure meeting with sponsor • Shares and tests development plan with colleagues • Checks progress periodically with sponsor and colleagues	Colleagues: • Broaden commitment to executive's plan • Support executive's development efforts

Conclusion

If you decide to embark on a coaching process, it can indeed be a thrilling adventure. The more you put into it (in terms of time, effort, openness, and willingness to question your assumptions and try new things), the more you will get out of it. The potential is for you to not only become more effective in your role at work but also to have more satisfaction in your life as a whole.

I hope that this book has helped prepare you to be an active and effective participant in your own coaching process. Don't be passive about the process. Join in and make sure that you get everything you want and need.

- Decide what your interest is in coaching and what outcomes you want

- Be prepared to address the prerequisites to performance improvement and to explore beyond the level of outward behavior

- Be proactive in selecting a coach and make sure that your coach is capable and has the necessary competencies

- Make sure that, at every stage, the basic activities described in this book occur, while still allowing for variation in coaches' styles

- Raise any issues or concerns that you have with your coach, and seek to diagnose and change what needs to be changed

Participating as a partner and not just as a recipient is also a model of a powerful way to engage with your colleagues, regardless of their relationship to you. Just engaging in the coaching process can shift your way of interacting with others to a more mindful and effective style.

Frequently Asked Questions

My coaching group is repeatedly asked to address several questions about executive coaching when talking with prospective clients and sponsors or during the coaching process itself. Answering these questions here might be a useful way to summarize some key points, as well as to address some concerns you may have now or in the future. The questions listed here are organized into sections: whether you need coaching, the coaching method and its rationale, how to select a coach, how the coaching process works, and how to evaluate a coaching project.

QUESTIONS ABOUT DETERMINING WHETHER YOU NEED COACHING

What are some questions to help determine whether I could benefit from coaching?

- Am I experiencing issues with performing my role or achieving my goals?

- Am I frequently frustrated because the effect I have on others is not what I intended?

- Am I involved in recurring conflicts?

- Was I disappointed in the feedback I received in a recent performance review?

- Did I fail to get a promotion I wanted?

- Did I recently make a transition to a new role?

- Am I having difficulty adjusting to a new job?

- Am I not getting the behavior or performance I expect from my colleagues or direct reports?

- Am I trying to change how my team operates?

- Am I interested in getting some authentic, but potentially tough, feedback about how others perceive my leadership?

- Am I prepared to make the effort to change my behavior?

What questions should I ask if my boss or HR manager suggests that I participate in coaching?

- What are the issues in my performance, results, or relationships that you are hoping coaching will address?

- What outcomes would you expect to see from coaching? How would you measure success or decide whether I'd made the desired changes?

- What do you see as the potential consequences of my participating in a successful coaching project? What would the consequences be if I did not participate?

- How will you help support my development?

QUESTIONS ABOUT THE RATIONALE FOR THE COACHING METHOD

Coaching seems very expensive and time-consuming. Why should I spend my resources this way, instead of on some other executive education?

- Developing executives is difficult. There are challenges in getting feedback, acknowledging the need for change, and adopting new behaviors. A training program is unlikely to get you past those hurdles, whereas a one-on-one coaching relationship can.

- In any case, you might not be willing to participate in training. Most senior executives avoid group training because they feel that it's too public. They might worry that attending training sessions with others at different hierarchical levels inhibits others from fully participating.

- Even if you participate in some training, coaching is essential to support the implementation of skills, tailor implementation to your style, overcome the hurdles you encounter, and internalize the training lessons.

Are some issues inappropriate to address with coaching, and why?

- If you need therapy, you should see a therapist, not a coach. For example, if you are facing a major life crisis or are experiencing significant adjustment issues in all areas of your life, a therapist would be better able to help you.

- If you have a fundamental lack of fit in your job, or if you have asked your colleagues what they expect and know you are not willing or able to produce it, then coaching will not be successful in the specific context of your current job. You may wish to contract for coaching to help you select a new career path or to be more effective in a future job. However, if someone is offering coaching with the expectation that you will improve performance in your current role, then to accept that coaching will just lead to continued frustration on all sides.

- If you feel coerced into participating in a coaching process, that process will not be helpful to you. You will not have the feelings of trust and openness that are required for a productive coaching relationship unless you feel that the coach is there to help you and that you are choosing to participate in your own interest.

QUESTIONS ABOUT SELECTING A COACH

What type of coach do I need? What are the differences between an executive coach, a personal coach, and a life coach?

- Executive coaches usually have some sort of dual contract with executives and their organizations and thus have dual objectives. One objective is to help executives understand and fulfill their personal goals and vision, and the other objective is to improve performance from the organizations' point of view. Executive coaching is typically funded by the organization.

- The terms *personal coach* and *life coach* are sometimes used interchangeably, but there can be a slight distinction. Personal coaches often focus on career goals, but strictly from the perspective of the individual. They can help the individual clarify vision, goals, career issues, and interests and act in many ways like a career counselor. Life coaches often go beyond career issues to help the individual clarify and achieve life goals in areas such as relationships, health and fitness, and personal priorities. Both types of coaching are usually funded by the individual. Personal and life coaching typically rely, if they use feedback at all, on career and personal style instruments filled out by the individual and perhaps a significant other. These coaches don't usually use 360-degree feedback, as their focus is more internal than external.

What type of education, training, or experience should I expect an effective coach to have?

- There is a lot of latitude here, but generally it is useful for coaches to have formal education in a relevant field such as business, psychology (either industrial-organizational, clinical, or counseling), or organizational behavior. A graduate degree in the field may be preferable.

- Specialized training can supplement an educational background that is not directly relevant. For example, coaches could have attended certificate programs in executive coaching or organizational change, such as those offered by the Gestalt Institute or Columbia University. Also, coaches should have specific training for the psychological instruments they use.

- Some coaches have had experience as managers or executives. That can be useful, as long as it does not lead them to see their role as giving advice or sharing expertise. The best experience is a lot of practice coaching various individuals in diverse organizations. Some experience with other kinds of organization development or training can also help coaches provide related support, such as teaching you skills or helping you lead change in your organization.

Does the coach need direct experience in my technical area or industry?

- Most managers feel that their organization's culture is different from others, but it is rarely so different that a skilled coach can't figure out the norms, language, and values fairly quickly. It does not hurt to have some experience in the technical area or industry, but it is not necessary to effectively play the coaching role.

Should personality match or mismatch influence the selection of a coach, and if so, how?

- Sometimes differences help. For example, laid-back, gentle, nonthreatening coaches can sometimes pierce the armor of hard-charging, aggressive executives more easily than forceful coaches, who can potentially provoke competitiveness or defensiveness.

- Sometimes similarities help. If coaches can empathize with your character issues, they can use that empathy to help. For example, coaches who have overcome their focus on rationality and being right can connect with executives who are challenged by this focus. One of the best coaches I know overcame a background of substance abuse and now helps executives who are themselves dealing with this issue.

Does it matter whether I work with a male or a female coach? If it does, how do I decide what's best for me?

- There is no right answer here, just different considerations. You should think about whether gender would make a difference in your typical comfort level. If you are more comfortable with a certain gender, then you should choose who would help you feel comfortable—just as you would choose based on other characteristics that would help you feel comfortable.

- If any of your coaching issues have to do with how you relate to men or women, then coaching can be a useful laboratory. In other words, you might wish to choose a coach of the gender that you typically have trouble with, so you can see and deal with these issues as they play out in your coaching relationship.

QUESTIONS ABOUT HOW THE PROCESS WORKS

What questions should I be asking during contracting?

- What is the organization's expectation of me? What is the coach's expectation of me? Do I feel I can meet these expectations?

- Am I prepared to hear tough feedback? Will I be able to do activities with others that may make me feel vulnerable, such as talk about my development, try new behaviors, or ask for feedback?

- How am I going to integrate the coaching process into my normal work? For example, how will I make sure that I can take the time to plan and debrief interactions? How will I incorporate discussions with colleagues about my development into my normal conversations with them?

- What are *all* my expectations—of the coach, sponsor, process, and outcomes?

FREQUENTLY ASKED QUESTIONS **129**

- Will my meetings with my coach be face-to-face or by telephone, or some combination of the two?

- When will the process end? If there is no firm end date, how will we decide when the process is completed?

How long should the coaching process last? Can it be too short or too long?

- There is no right answer to this. However, a duration of less than six months makes it difficult to deal with the ebbs and flows of change and to do the practice that is needed for you to internalize the new behaviors and make them your own.

- On the other hand, staying in a coaching relationship too long can create its own problems. Working with your coach for longer than two years may suggest that you are too dependent on him or her, unless you have experienced significant life or role changes that required a shift in the coaching focus.

What should I say to my colleagues about the process? Should I tell them what I'm doing and why?

- You may feel you shouldn't say anything to them. But actually, being transparent about why you're participating in coaching can be a very powerful and different way of interacting with your colleagues.

- All you need to tell them is that you want to improve your leadership effectiveness, and that you will want their help and support. You will be amazed at the amount of goodwill you will receive.

What activities should not be part of the process? Are there things a coach should not do?

- A coach should not do therapy or push you to an emotional place that he or she is not equipped to manage.

- A coach should not shadow-manage, as did a coach of my acquaintance who regularly took her client's place leading the weekly team meetings when the client was absent from work.

- A coach should not be a spy for the executive's boss, or for anyone else. People will try to use the coach to triangulate by talking to the coach about their issues with other people, often hoping that the coach will pass on this information. The coach should not enable people to take this easy way out. Part of the coach's job is to help people handle their relationship issues more directly, and so he or she must encourage those people to deliver their own messages.

- A coach should not foster dependence.

- A coach should not get involved in the content of your business decisions.

What information about my career plans should I share, or not share, with the coach?

- Share whatever you believe is relevant. If you are considering leaving your job, that may be relevant. If you are experiencing a crisis in your personal life, that may be relevant.

- If you are concerned that the coach will inappropriately share this information with others, of course you should not share it. However, if that is the case, you should probably not be in a relationship with that coach.

How much should I discuss with my coach about issues that don't seem directly related to performance?

Executive coaching is about improving performance, but doing this requires dealing with you as a whole person. Many issues can arise during coaching that do not seem to be related to performance issues, yet they are. If you have any of the issues from the following list, they will probably emerge, and should emerge, during your coaching work, and you should be prepared to deal with them.

- Work–life balance and the state of your personal relationships
- Addiction and substance abuse
- Religion and spirituality
- Image and physical presence
- Difficult life histories

What should I expect to pay for a coaching engagement?

- Most executive coaching is billed on a project basis, and most coaches will not charge you for every second that they are talking with you because they want to encourage you to use them.

- The project fee depends on the design and intensity of your coaching process. At one end is a brief coaching process, lasting three months or so, for as little as $10,000. This design is made possible by limiting the number of interviews and possibly having the executive collect some of the feedback instead of the coach. In addition, the executive must typically focus on fewer development issues. At the other end, I have heard of individual coaching projects costing $150,000 to $200,000, although those projects are most likely multiyear engagements. The average cost is probably around $40,000 to $60,000 for a one-year engagement. It is also common that coaching projects with the most senior executives are more expensive than those for less senior executives, because of additional constraints created by the executive's role and visibility.

QUESTIONS ABOUT EVALUATING COACHING

How should I measure the effectiveness of the coaching process?

- Choose measures that relate to how your use of new behaviors helped you accomplish business goals.

- Look for observable behavior changes on your part.

- Note if and how others respond differently to you.

- Consider all possible effects of your new behaviors on organizational success.

How quickly should I expect to see change, and what changes should I expect to see?

- You should be able to try some new behaviors immediately. For example, if feedback reveals something others expect of you, you may find that it is easy to incorporate those new behaviors.

- When you learn a new skill, change will take slightly longer.

- Change will take the longest when your challenge is to build a broader perspective. For example, let's say that you would like to consult others more before making decisions.

  - If you learned through their feedback that specific individuals would prefer that you consult them, and you hadn't realized this before, you might be able to change this behavior easily and start consulting them immediately.

  - However, if you lack the skill needed to identify people's interests in your decision, then developing this behavior will take more training and practice.

  - Furthermore, underlying this symptom may be a challenge of perspective. You may need to better appreciate the value of others' input, to think more deeply about whose input might be relevant in the different decisions you make, or to consider how your decisions will affect your various colleagues. Developing beyond the limits of your current perspective will probably take sustained time and effort, and active coaching, for you to see situations differently.

  - Finally, changing your behavior might be most challenging if your actions are shaped by your character. For example, if you don't seek others' input because you think your answer is the best, you have a need to be right, or you are threatened by the idea that others' input might be valuable, then it will be more difficult for you to change in a way that lasts. In this case, you still might be able to change, but your behavior might be inconsistent or people might see it as phony. It's not impossible to change in this situation, but you should expect difficulty and backsliding.

What should I do if I fall back into behaviors or styles that I thought the coaching had changed?

- What you should *not* do is feel disheartened. Backsliding is inevitable, especially when you are under stress or when your buttons get pushed.

- What you *should* do instead is, first, understand what triggered the backsliding. Did someone do or say something to you that led you to react? What did the action mean to you?

- Once you understand your trigger, you can develop a plan for anticipating backsliding before it occurs. The trigger can become a red flag, and once you've seen it, you can become very mindful about how you react to the situation.

- Finally, after an episode of backsliding, it is very important to "clean up": acknowledge what has happened, apologize if you feel that is appropriate, and find out what you can do to correct the consequences.

What steps should I take if I have concerns about how the coaching process is working?

- First, identify what has happened to cause your concern.

- Second, determine what you want to change and how.

- Finally, talk with your coach and try to negotiate a solution that will address your concerns.

What steps should I take if I believe I need to end the process with a particular coach?

- Again, it's critical to talk to your coach. People become dissatisfied with their coaches for several reasons. Sometimes, there are legitimate issues with the coach that cannot be repaired, and perhaps the relationship does need to end. More frequently, this kind of dissatisfaction is a reaction to the challenge and discomfort of activities required to create real behavior change. A good coach will work with you to determine the cause of your dissatisfaction and help you decide if it makes sense to terminate the engagement.

- You will also need to talk with your sponsor and agree on the implications of this decision.

Resources

ORIGINAL CCL® RESEARCH ON EXECUTIVE DEVELOPMENT

Kaplan, Robert, with Wilfred Drath and Joan Kofodimos. *Beyond Ambition: How Driven Managers Can Lead Better and Live Better.* San Francisco: Jossey-Bass, 1991.

The character of executives and the typical deeply rooted issues that make executive development challenging and that necessitate coaching.

Kaplan, Robert, Wilfred Drath, and Joan Kofodimos. "High Hurdles: The Challenge of Executive Self Development." *Academy of Management Executive* 1, no. 3 (1987): 195–205.

How the elevated position of executives poses barriers to continued learning and development.

Kofodimos, Joan. "Using Biographical Methods to Understand Managerial Style and Character." *Journal of Applied Behavioral Science* 26, no. 4 (1990): 433–459.

The principles behind the design of 360-degree interview feedback.

WORK–PERSONAL LIFE BALANCE

Kofodimos, Joan. *Balancing Act: How Managers Can Integrate Successful Careers and Fulfilling Personal Lives.* San Francisco: Jossey-Bass, 1993.

The underlying dynamics of work and personal life that contribute to performance issues.

DEVELOPMENT AND BROADENED PERSPECTIVE

Goodman, Robert. "Coaching Senior Executives for Effective Business Leadership: The Use of Adult Developmental Theory as a Basis for Transformative Change." In *Executive Coaching, Practices and Perspectives,* **edited by Catherine Fitzgerald and Jennifer Garvey Berger, 135–153. Mountain View, CA: Davies-Black Publishing, 2002.**

How the coaching conversation is specifically designed to help broaden an executive's perspective.

Kegan, Robert, and Lisa Lahey. *How the Way We Talk Can Change the Way We Work.* San Francisco: Jossey-Bass, 2001.

Breaks down the elements of the process that coaches use (or that you can use yourself) for transcending resistant areas of attitude and behavior.

GENERAL GUIDELINES FOR EXECUTIVE COACHING, CURRENT RESEARCH, AND SO ON

Executive Coaching Forum. "TECF—The Executive Coaching Forum." www.theexecutivecoachingforum.com/index.htm.

Web site of an organization dedicated to advancing the standards and practices of executive coaching. A gold mine of material, updated regularly.

Index

ability to learn, 11
assessment of coaching, 112–113
authentic feedback: lack of, 14; procuring and providing of, 17–18

barriers to change, 10–11
behaviors: backsliding of, 106–107, 133; changing of, 18, 58, 104, 132–133; implementing of, 82, 101; interpersonal abrasiveness, 24; micromanagement, 24; new types of, 31; obstacles to, 101; old types of, 106; resistance to, 105–106, 110; self-perceptions of, 104; soliciting information about, 75; by sponsors, 34; troublesome types of, 24
"brain trust," 14
broadening of perspective, 7–8

change: barriers to, 10–11; behaviors, 18, 58, 82, 104; benefits of, 18; colleagues' expectation for, 33; effective management of, 25; paths for, 18; preparing others for, 94–97, 109; resistance to, 25–26; time required for results of, 132–133
clarity of purpose, 5–6, 98–99, 109
closure stage: activities of, 111–119; meeting, 118; objectives of, 111–112; output of, 119; summary of, 120
coach: assessment of, 47–48, 70; background of, 46; behaviors and activities not allowed by, 129–130; being authentic with, 32; challenges by, 40–41; competencies of, 39–45, 47–48; confidentiality by, 43–44, 52, 55; credentials of, 46–47; debriefing with, 102, 110; description of, 39; empathy by, 127; expectations of, 55; experience of, 126–127; feedback by, 41–42; "fit" with, 45–46; gender of, 128; meeting with, 54–58, 69; non-performance issues discussed with, 130–131; organizational dynamics and, 46; perception of, 40–41; questions frequently asked about, 125–128; roles not appropriate for, 45; selection of, 125–128; sponsor's meeting with, 52–54, 57–58; support given by, 40–41; as therapist, 45; training experience of, 126; understanding by, 40
coaching: activities associated with, 12; agreement for, 82; appropriateness of, 58–59; assessment of, 112–113; balancing support and challenge in, 40–41; change barriers identified through, 10–11; clarity of purpose achieved through, 5–6; concerns about, 133; contract for, 61–68; contracting phase of. See contracting phase; costs of, 131; cyclical approach to, 11; duration of, 129; ending of, 134; evaluation of, 131–134; executive development strategies, 17–19; factors that affect the success of, 37; goals for, 3, 54; impact of, 111; implementation phase of. See implementation phase; insight